Wm Tod Helmuth

A RECORD

OF THE

SURGICAL CLINICS

OF

HELD AT THE

N. Y. HOMŒOPATHIC MEDICAL COLLEGE

DURING THE SESSION OF 1874-'75.

—BY—

PHILETUS J. STEPHENS.

TO WHICH IS ADDED A SYNOPSIS OF THE CLINICS OF 1873-'74.

New York:
1875.

To

The Faculty and Trustees

OF THE

New York Homœopathic Medical College

THIS WORK

IS RESPECTFULLY SUBMITTED,

BY

PHILETUS J. STEPHENS.

PREFACE.

DURING the last session of the New York Homœopathic Medical College the undersigned was often struck with the brilliancy of the Surgical Clinics, and then determined, if he were spared another term, he would publish these Clinics, not only for the advancement of the college in which they were delivered, but for the good of the Homœopathic cause generally. The method of conducting the lecture is as follows: the patients are sent from the Dispensary to the Amphitheatre and are introduced one by one to the class.

There is not any selection of cases, or opportunity afforded for the lecturer to examine the patient, make up his diagnosis, select his remedy and prepare what apparatus is best; and for these reasons the author has endeavored to give the record in full, that the Clinics may appear, not dressed up with rhetoric and illustration, *but as they really took place.* The author also desires, at the request of Prof. Helmuth, to state that he (Prof. Helmuth) was unaware that these Clinics were being reported *verbatim* as they fell from his lips, until the session was almost over, and then he was for the first time made aware of the fact by the printed proof sheets being presented for his inspection.

The author conceived that by keeping the matter entirely private during the term that he could more certainly offer to the students, the faculty of the college and the public the method in which Clinical Surgery is taught in the New York Homœopathic College, which, he conceives, has no superior in this country.

PHILETUS J. STEPHENS.

SURGICAL CLINICS OF 1874-'75

OF THE

New York Homœopathic Medical College.

THE Session of the New York Homœopathic Medical College for 1874 and '75 commenced October 10th, 1874, in the large and elegant Amphitheatre, under most favorable auspices.

At the first Clinic there were present more than one hundred students, and more patients applied than could be attended to; indeed, throughout the entire session, this has been the case.

These Clinics are always lively, pleasant and attractive to students as well as physicians, and give entire satisfaction; they sparkle with humor, and reflect great credit upon Professor Wm. Tod Helmuth, who, we think, proves himself a perfect master of the art of surgery. The chief peculiarity of the Clinics are the promiscuous and rapidly given "quizzes."

Surgical Clinic of October 10.

A boy being brought in with his arm in a splint, Professor Wm. Tod Helmuth looked at it for a moment, and commenced to question the class as follows:

What do we understand by the term fracture? Answer.—A solution of continuity of the Osseous System; or, in other words, a separation or breakage of the bones, by various causes, both direct and indirect. A fracture may be known by pain, loss of power, and crepitus, or peculiar sensation from rubbing the ends of the broken bones together.

What various divisions of fractures are recognized by surgeons? Simple, Compound, Comminuted, Impacted, Complete, and Incomplete Fracture.

What is a simple fracture? Is when the bone is broken at one point, without any wound of the flesh.

What is a compound fracture? Is one where there is a breakage of the bone, with a wound of the soft parts.

What is a comminuted fracture? Is one where the bone has been broken in more than one place, or cracked in many places.

What is a compound comminuted fracture? One where the bone is splintered, or the breakage of bones into several fragments with accompanying wounds of the soft parts.

What is an impacted fracture? One in which one extremity or portion of the bone is wedged or driven into the other.

What is a complete fracture? One in which there is an entire separation of the bone.

What is an incomplete fracture? One in which there is but a partial division of the osseous material.

What terms are used to designate the directions in which the separation may occur? Transverse, longitudinal, oblique or serrated fracture.

What is a transverse fracture? One which is directly across the bone.

What is a longitudinal fracture? One which runs lengthwise of the bone.

What is an oblique fracture? One in which the line of fracture runs from side to side in an oblique direction, or obliquely to the base of the bone.

What is reduction? Setting a fracture: that is, bringing the ends of the broken bones together and adjusting them to each other in their natural position, embracing extension, counter extension, and coaptation.

What is extension? The taking hold of the limb below the fracture and making traction from the body.

What is counter extension? Traction above the fracture towards the body, or steadying the body.

Must this opposite traction be done at the same time? Yes; to overcome the force of the muscles, which contract and draw the ends of the broken bone over each other and so shorten the limb.

Sometimes extension and counter extension are not required.

What is coaptation? Adjusting the ends of the bones to each other.

What would you do with a fractured limb? Would set the bones: that is, restore the fragments as nearly as possible to their natural position, keeping the ends of the broken bone in contact by mechanical contrivances, such as bandages, pads, splints and rollers, so as to maintain them in such position that nature may have a fair chance to unite the broken bone together.

What next would you do? Prevent or allay constitutional or local disturbances.

Fracture of the Humerus.

JOHN A. POWERS, *Aged Five Years.*

The first case to-day is one of fracture. By fracture, I mean a breakage of the bone, or ossific matter—a solution of continuity in any of the bony structures of the human body.

It is always of great importance when looking at a fracture and making your diagnosis to find out, if you can, the position of the patient at the time that the injury was received. In a patient so young as this we will be unable to discover how he fell, whether on his arm or not.

The next thing to be done when a patient is brought to you with a fracture is to look for the three signs thereof, which are almost always present. These three symptoms are crepitus, preternatural mobility and deformity. There are other symptoms, but these are the three generally found, and these demand attention.

It is always important in a case of fracture to try to ascertain, if we can, if crepitus be present—and by the term crepitus we understand the sound which is produced and emitted when the fractured extremities of a bone are rubbed together, or the grating together of the two ends of a fractured bone, and the peculiar sensation that is felt by a surgeon during a careful examination.

True crepitus, in itself, is always diagnostic of a fracture. When I say crepitus, I mean true crepitus. You must be careful not to mistake true for false crepitus, which you often find in that peculiar rubbing noise that may be distinctly heard in the irritated sheaths of tendons and joints, or from accumulation of air in the tissues. True crepitus is not only felt, but often heard. It resembles, as closely as possible, to the ear the sound produced by the rubbing together of two pieces of loaf sugar. If you have a patient brought to you with supposed fracture, and you can find true crepitus, you do not want anything else.

You must also bear in mind an important fact, that a fracture may exist without crepitus. Thus, in the so-called impacted fractures, or in those where strong muscular contraction draw asunder the fragments, there may not be a trace of the sound, and I would have this point strongly impressed upon the mind.

Preternatural Mobility.—This symptom is generally present in fractures, although, in the bones of the leg and forearm, when one bone only is the seat of injury, the increased motion may be very slight, as may also be noticed in the impacted variety; but by grasping the fractured bone above the contusion and holding it firmly and moving the lower portion of the bone in a lateral direction, an unnatural motion may be generally observed.

This preternatural mobility may also be difficult to recognize—especially when the bony lesion takes place in the vicinity of a joint and there is much contusion of the soft parts which may be torn or lacerated.

Preternatural mobility is more frequently found in the shafts of bones than in fractures in the vicinity of the joints, because when you have a fracture in the vicinity of the joint there is generally so much swelling that there is less mobility than usual. But if you have a fracture in the shaft of the humerus, or if you have both bones of the forearm broken, then, of course, there will be mobility, when, under ordinary circumstances, there would be none.

We have not time now to enter into a discussion of fractures and the different methods of treatment. It is very interesting, but would occupy too much time.

It is always well when you have to treat a fracture to act with the utmost delicacy, otherwise you are very apt to bruise the tissues.

Here is a fracture which is somewhere in the vicinity of the elbow joint—and fractures in the vicinity of the elbow joint are sometimes the most difficult that you have to deal with. I think that Gross says in his work that he never approaches a surgical case with as much fear and misgiving as he does fractures in the vicinity of the elbow, no matter how slight, because in eight cases out of ten they are liable to be followed with a certain amount of deformity. More or less stiffness in the joint is a result which, even under the most careful treatment, cannot be prevented.

We must find out exactly where this fracture is. In the first place I support the hand and turn it in this way (supinating). Now, I know very well that the neck of the radius is not broken, because if it was the head of the bone would not move between my fingers. If the head of the radius were broken off I could not move it in the way that I am now doing.

The next thing we do is to lift the hand up in this way (illustrating). Then I feel for the olecranon process on the other side of the elbow, and I find that it is intact.

This boy has a fracture of the *external condyle.*

When you come to diagnose fractures about the elbow be extremely careful about your prognosis. There are frequently suits for malpractice on account of fractures about the elbow. There has been a recent case at Paterson, concerning which I have been consulted. Therefore I say that in the treatment of fractures about the joints you must always be exceedingly careful how you give an opinion.

I will remark in respect to this patient that he will have a pretty quick recovery, but that he may have stiffness in the joint. The reason for that stiffness I will explain to you hereafter, when we come to understand the process of repair, and the inflammatory action which results from an injury of this character. Inflammatory action may extend itself into the cavity of the joint, and a certain amount of plastic matter be effused, which will result in spurious anchylosis.

In a case like this the best dressing is a posterior rectangular splint. You can make it out of a segar box.

The chances for the recovery of this child are better than they would be if he were older. There will not be so much likelihood of trouble at the joint.

It is a question with a great many surgeons as to whether a bandage should be applied next to the skin before putting on a splint. Of course, there are many who say that a bandage should be so applied, and give as a reason that, while it controls muscular action, it also affords an equable and even support to the part. That is all very true in its way. On the other hand, those who are in favor of the non-application of a bandage next to the skin give it as their opinion that it certainly arrests the circulation. No matter how lightly the bandage is put on, the circulation may be arrested; therefore, it is a matter which is open to the judgment of every discriminating surgeon whether or not he shall apply a bandage before he applies the splint. In a case like this I would suppose it better not to put a bandage next to the skin at all: but if we have adhesive plaster handy we will secure the arm in proper position simply by the use of the posterior rectangular splint with adhesive straps.

It is hardly my province now to enter into the anatomy of the lower end of the humerus, although it is very important to know what muscles (flexors and extensors) there are, and how they are attached; but we will defer this until some other time.

It is important for you to recollect that the deposit of osseous matter does not take place in a fracture until the seventh or eighth day; and, therefore, you are to apply your splints and keep the parts in good position for seven or eight days, and then it is well to examine the fracture again. If the parts are in position apply a permanent bandage. But if you come to your patient the day after the first dressing and find that there is a tendency to swelling, and that the nails begin to look blue, take the bandage off, or else nick it; there are more arms and legs lost by surgeons through tight bandaging than from bad treatment of the fractures. If you could examine into the literature of surgery you would see that in a great many cases the loss of a limb has been occasioned by tight bandaging. It seems to have been a notion of the surgeons in the olden time that when they applied a bandage they must use a good deal of force, to wrap it tightly around, in order to keep the bone in position. This is a wrong principle from beginning to end—a moderately tight bandage, such as you see here, is all that is necessary.

We will first pack this splint well with cotton.

Doctors make more mistakes, ten to one, than surgeons. You may put that down as a rule. The difference is just this: the doctors bury their errors under the sod, while a surgeon's mistakes are held up to posterity.

This boy will probably come back to us this day week. We will then have his arm undressed and look at it, to see how it does. The bandage is now put on quite loosely, but it will keep his arm in that position. Even now there may be some little tendency to swelling of the fingers. It is always better to watch such fractures closely.

In the case over in Paterson, in which I was called to testify the other day, the bandage had been applied quite tightly, gangrene had resulted and the arm been amputated. That was three years ago. They buried the arm in the earth. One man swore that the olecranon process was broken off. Another physician said that the head of the radius was severed. Another that the coronoid process of the ulna was fractured, and others that the internal condyle of the humerus was separated. They said that they had the bones to prove it. "There was no getting around the bones;" so they dug up the arm a year and a half after it was buried, but all these parts had separated, because the epiphyses had not united with the shaft, and the long burial had consequently separated these parts. There were so many conflicting opinions about it that it seems rather doubtful whether the bone was broken at all.

In the treatment of fractures we employ two forces in setting the bone; one of these forces is called "extension," the other counter extension. Extension is always made in a direction *from* the body, and the counter extension is always made in a direction *towards* the body. In order to reduce a fracture a considerable amount of extension and counter extension may be employed. The object of this is to overcome the action of certain muscles which, being inserted below the seat of fracture, have a tendency to make the bones "ride" one on the other.

Prof. Gross speaks of fractures as follows: "If I were called upon to testify under oath what branch I regard as the most trying and the most difficult to practice successfully and creditably, I would unhesitatingly assert fractures."

This indicates the importance of thoroughly understanding the subject.

Large Nævus.

IDA TELLER, *Aged Five Months.*

This case is one that came from the Surgical Hospital under the charge of Dr. Thompson.

It is known as nævus, which is an enlargement of the capillary vessels; nævi are flat, slightly elevated, and of a red or purplish hue; they are usually small, and occur most frequently on the head, face, neck and arms. The contained blood may be arterial or venous, or a mixture of the two.

As a general rule their growth does not attain a size much larger than an egg.

The appearance is sometimes called "mother's mark." A true aneurism is different from a nævus. A nævus is an enlargement of the capillaries of the arteries and veins, whereas a true aneurism by anastomosis is nothing more nor less than an enlargement of the arterial capillaries rather than of the veins.

Nævi are sometimes very difficult to treat. They are generally found at birth. In fact I have never yet heard of one which was not present at birth. They vary in size, from that of the head of a large pin to several inches in diameter. They are caused by an enlargement of the smaller blood vessels of the part, and by an increased action of the heart and vessels tending to throw the blood to that part. The capillaries are enlarged, and, not having the power of passing the blood through them, the parts become enlarged and reddened. These nævi are always worse when the child cries, because then an additional amount of blood is thrown into the tissues.

There are a variety of methods employed for the relief of these nævi. A simple nævus may be removed, when it consists of a red spot, by vaccination, or by application of collodion with pressure. When situated over a bone the tumor may be treated by compression with pads of ivory or other hard substances. Or you take a needle and thread it with an ordinary piece of silk, dip the silk in dilute nitric acid, run the needle beneath the nævus and let the ends of the ligature hang. Injections of persulphate or perchloride of iron, sulphate of zinc, acetate of iron, matico, tannin and ether astringents may prove useful.

Dr. Gross speaks highly of the topical application of Vienna paste. Dr. Valentine Mott advised puncture with red hot needles, or acupressure pins. Perhaps the best method of treating nævi is by electrolysis or galvano puncture. Many successful cures are on record. Some surgeons prefer nitrate of silver or the actual cautery. Or you may apply collodion over the surface. This has a tendency, from its contractile powers, to force out the blood, and it is a very excellent dressing after an operation for nævus has been performed. Another method is the introduction of pins deep down under the tumor, and strangling the growth by ligature underneath the pins. There is another method—by passing a double thread under the base of the tumor, leaving the strands hanging out in opposite directions, then passing the needle through at right angles, cutting the strands, and tying those above and those below. Another practice is to ligate the main vessel giving the supply of blood. I have myself employed this treatment for a nævus occupying half the side of a child's head. The growth had attained the size of half an ordinary sized melon, for which I ligated the common carotid below the omo-hyoid after failure by other means. At first the tumor diminished one half, then remained stationary for a time, and has since disappeared. But one of the best methods known you will see employed to-day. This child has been operated on twice with a red hot iron, the marks of which you can see.

This nævus is a large one, and is in a very peculiar position—on the nose. It is not in a position where the parts are all smooth, and you have a plain surface to work upon, but it is so situated as to require a great deal of care in the operation, and the process itself is by no means devoid of danger.

The operation which Dr. Thompson proposes to perform is this: He has prepared a round needle—and the reason that a round one is used is because these broad, cutting needles often give rise to a great deal of hemorrhage; the needle is very sharp, and it is threaded with a long piece of silk thread (made of new braided silk, which will not kink or break), about six feet in length, one half of which is black and the other white. Thread the needle upon the middle of this cord. I will give you the history of the operation, and then you will see it done. You enter the needle at about one quarter of an inch from the end of the tumor, and pass the needle several times beneath the nævus. The loops should be three quarters of an inch apart and the last one be brought out through the healthy tissue, beyond the tumor. Thus we have double loops—one white and one black—on each side. Cut the white loops on one side and the black on the other, or at the top you keep all the thread of one color and at the bottom you keep all the thread of the other color. Then tie firmly the white threads on one side and the black on the other side, and the nævus is effectually strangulated.

The prognosis in the case cannot be said to be remarkably favorable, but nevertheless we will have to do the best we can. But it is certain that unless an operation is performed there can be no help for the child. A profuse hemorrhage would soon result. This is the only means left to save the life of this child. It is a perfectly well understood matter between the parents and the operator that they assume all the responsibility in this case. The father has been told all about it. He knows that it is a dangerous operation, but he wishes it performed because he knows that it is the only thing that can be done, and he is willing to assume all the responsibility; he is anxious to have the child live; there is no doubt of that. It is in just such cases that surgery steps in. The question arises—Is there anything in *medicine* that will do this child good? Will all the medicine of all the schools be able to cure this nævus? I do not think there is a chance for it in medicine. When the physicians get into trouble they often come to the surgeon, and when the surgeon fails there is no power on earth to save.

This nævus has been extending daily. In this operation we shall use an anæsthetic. You all know, gentlemen, that anæsthesia is the next step to death. It simulates death. It takes but a very little more of the anæsthetic agent to step from a previous life into death. Therefore, it behooves us when we would administer such an agent to select that one which is the best. When I say the "best," I mean that agent which is safest, and not that which is the quickest, unless the quickest is the safest. Of course, you know that the discovery of ether belongs to America. The discovery of chloroform, or, more properly speaking, the introduction of chloroform, belongs to England. Wells and Morton claim priority of discovery in this country, while Simpson lays claim to it in England.

The American Medical Association, at its meeting held at Washington in 1870, passed the following resolution: "Dr. Horace Wells, of Hartford, Conn., was the discoverer of anæsthesia." Very distinguished gentlemen, while giving the discovery of *nitrous* oxide anæsthesia to Dr. Wells, accord priority of the sulphuric ether anæsthesia to Dr. Wm. T. G. Morton, of Boston. Not many years since one of the greatest surgeons, Velpeau, of Paris, told his medical pupils that although enthusiasts at different times had vainly imagined that some means might be adopted to allay the pain of surgical operations, yet that such an idea was entirely chimerical, and must ever remain so. The thing, he said, was impossible, and all hope of it but a vain delusion. In five years from that hour Velpeau, of Paris, amputated limbs and performed other grave operations whilst his willing patients were sleeping from anæsthesia. An American dentist, Dr. Horace Wells, of Hartford, Conn., conceived the idea of preventing the pain of surgical operations, and took the ether himself to have a tooth extracted. He devoted years to this discovery, with an enthusiasm not excelled among ancient or modern inventors, but was ridiculed and abused. He was so disheartened by ingratitude that he died by his own hands in 1848. Dr. Morton finally died, discouraged, disheartened and penniless. His remains rest in Mount Auburn Cemetery, near Boston, "without a stone to mark the spot." What a homily could be read on this history! What a lesson does it teach us!

There can be no doubt when we compare the symptoms occasioned by the use of the two anæsthetics, that chloroform is decidedly the more pleasant. Patients succumb to its influence a great deal quicker. There is none of the excitability which attends the use of ether, and it probably takes less than one fourth the time to chloroform a patient that it does to bring him under the influence of ether. In the one case the danger to life is comparatively great, while in the other it is reduced to a minimum. The temptation to the surgeon to administer chloroform is very strong, when he knows—as is generally the case—that a patient will go through the various stages of intoxication if ether be given.

Chloroform will very often bring a patient under anæsthetic influence with extreme rapidity, but you scarcely know when your patients are in a dangerous condition if it be administered; and the deaths are numerous that can be attributed to its use. Although I have given chloroform a thousand times or more without accident, on two occasions I was on the verge of losing the lives of patients—once in Buffalo and once in St. Louis—and I have abjured the use of this agent from that time to the present as a general rule. I only use it occasionally. Ether produces all that we want, and if it is properly applied, can be made almost as serviceable as chloroform. If, before taking the ether, the patient is allowed to fast, and a stimulant given twenty minutes before the inhalation commences, the ether takes effect with much

2

greater rapidity. If you do not desire to give stimulants in the shape of brandy or whiskey, you can give ten grains of the bromide of potash, which accelerates the influence of ether with most remarkable facility, and then there is no danger. I say that it is better to have the trouble, if any, with the patients alive on the table, and let them squeal, and vomit and kick if they like, and talk all kinds of nonsense, and occupy a great deal of your time—it is better to have your trouble then, than have it in a court of law afterwards, when the operator may be subjected to the most distressing self-reproaches if he has happened to lose a patient. I do not believe that any feeling ever passes through the mind of the conscientious surgeon which is more painful to himself, or renders him more miserable, than that of seeing a patient die on the table, while taking an anæsthetic—particularly when he knows, or thinks, or believes that if he had used another agent the result might have been different. There are, however, some surgeons who prefer to use the nitrous oxide to any other anæsthetic. It is an excellent method so long as it lasts, but it is too evanescent in its effect. It passes off in a very short space of time, and if you were to use it in general practice you would require a dray to go behind your carriage to carry the bags. For short operations it is very nice, but for tedious ones, it is not desirable, unless in a hospital where you can manufacture it, and then it is necessary to have it always made pure.

This child has been twice tried with chloroform, but the effects were bad; it lost its breath immediately; therefore it is better to use ether, and take a longer time, if necessary.

The parents state that this nævus was as large as a three cent piece when the child was born, and that when it was three or four weeks old the nævus was twice treated with a hot iron. This treatment is not desirable, as it is not so successful as the other methods I have referred to.

(Dr. Thompson then continued the operation.)

You will notice in this operation that the black threads come together, and the white ones also. We draw and tie the threads very tightly.

This operation is a very serious one, and we do not know exactly what will be the result. We hope, however, it is for the best.

Surgical Clinic, October 17.

Epithelioma.

PATRICK MURPHY, *Aged Eighty-five.*

Here is a patient brought to us from Bridgeport, Conn., for treatment for Epithelioma, or Epithelial Cancer, which is one of the mildest forms of cancer, and affects often the lower lip, as in the present case.

Some authors have styled this disease semi-malignant, or cancroid. In fact, it occupies a somewhat anomalous position, closely resembling innocent growths in cell structure, while in all other respects it is essentially malignant. Gross is inclined to think that it is "merely a form of scirrhus, modified in its character by the nature of the structure in which it occurs." It was formerly classed with lupus, but the later pathologists regard the latter as belonging to ulcers rather than tumors.

In regard to the causes of this disease but little is known. According to Paget, only one twentieth of the cases are referable to hereditary taint. External injury, long continued pressure and local irritation, may serve as exciting causes; for example, epithelioma of the lips may be induced by the pressure of the pipe, and the "chimney sweeper's cancer" is supposed to be caused by the irritation of soot lodged in the folds of the scrotum.

Epithelioma attacks men more frequently than women, and seldom occurs before the age of thirty-five or forty. It generally affects mucous and cutaneous tissues, especially the lips, tongue and face; but it may also invade deeply seated structures, and be found in the bones, muscles, lymphatics, liver, lungs scrotum, anus and penis.

It generally begins as a small wart, crack or tubercle on the skin, hard, movable, and tender on pressure. As it advances in growth it may assume several different shapes, sometimes consisting of small rounded masses, half imbedded in the skin; sometimes projecting in warty, cauliflower-like excrescences of a florid color, and extreme vascularity. Again, the tumor may assume a conical shape, and be covered by a thick laminated scab, like syphilitic rupia; and, lastly, these morbid growths may be pendulous, and attached to the integument by narrow bases.

On dissection epithelial cancer is found to consist of a firm, grayish or white substance, possessing considerable vascularity; unlike the varieties previously described, it has no stroma.

According to Druitt, "Microscopical examinations show:

1. The epidermic layer to be composed of epithelium, arranged in concentric layers around and between the papillæ.
2. The papillæ and dermis are composed of white, intermingled with yellow fibrous tissue, everywhere abundantly infiltrated with epithelial cells, and with their nuclei and fibroplastic matter. In the papillæ, the epithelium is seen to be arranged symmetrically in concentric layers amongst the scanty fibrous elements, and this arrangement may penetrate to some depth within the cutis, from which elongated and imbricated rolls of epithelium somewhat resembling the heads of young asparagus, can be extricated.
3. Within the cutis and subjacent tissue the epithelium is found sometimes in concentric pellets like comedones or grubs, or inspissated contents of sebaceous follicles, sometimes in rings formed within obstructed ducts or follicles, but usually in large, irregular quantities infiltrated amongst the fibres of the cutis and of the subcutaneous areolar tissue."

The cancer cells which Druitt describes as epithelial, differ greatly from those of scirrhus and encephaloid; in fact, they closely resemble the cells of pavement epithelium, they may be "round, oval, angular, fusiform or elongated," and they generally contain one or two nuclei, sometimes they are arranged in layers, and again they may be enclosed in cysts. Upon pressure, the cut surface of the cancer yields a clear serous fluid containing cells, nuclei, oil globules, and crystals of cholestearine.

In its growth, epithelioma gradually attacks and infiltrates all surrounding structures. At length ulceration sets in, the surface cracks at several points, and there exudes a purulent, sanious fluid, which dries in a scab, this is soon thrown off as a slough, and we see a deep, excavated ulcer, with hard base, and rough, irregular edges, surrounded by warty fungoid growths. There is an exceedingly foetid, corrosive discharge, and sometimes profuse hemorrhage is caused by ulceration into a blood vessel. The sore shows no disposition to heal ; the disease gradually extends to adjacent tissues, and integument, muscles and bones are alike involved in the destructive process. The pain is sharp, burning and lancinating; the constitutional symptoms are well pronounced, but, as a rule, the cachexia appears later than in the other varieties.*

After further examination of the case Prof. Helmuth continued as follows:

Epithelioma is a disease affecting the cells of the papillæ in different portions of the body, which become elevated, enlarged, readily bleeding, and finally become ulcerous. There are two distinct species of epithelioma, one of which is cutaneous and the other of which is deep. There is also another variety in which these growths become so large, and bleed so readily, and increase and grow in such a manner that they are called vegetating epithelioma. We find this class described under the name of cauliflower excrescence. A microscopical examination of the epithelioma discharge shows a closer resemblance to the epithelial scales of the body than those found in the malignant forms of cancer. Recollect this one thing, before I go any further—that one of the differences between cancer or a malignant tumor, and an innocent tumor, consists in the fact that the one is heterologous, or has tissues and cells not found ordinarily in the human body, while the innocent forms of tumors possess cells and structures similar to those found in the body. It seems as if this epithelioma were a variety betwixt the two—more malignant than the fibrous growth, yet not so malignant as the encephaloid, and other varieties of cancer ; and that its cell formation bears a closer resemblance to the healthy tissues of the body than any other variety of the so-called malignant formations.

An epithelioma is less likely to return than others ; and when operated upon quite early, if the glands are not involved and the patient is put under correct treatment afterwards, even if you cannot cure, you can postpone the disease for years. After the epithelial growth has been removed we continue internal

---

* The description of Epithelioma here inserted is taken from "Helmuth's Surgery."

methods of treatment for the cure of the disease, or the eradication of it from the system. The old fashioned doctrine that cancer is hereditary or constitutional, begins to shake at its foundation. The microscope has begun to uproot many of these older notions; and it is thought that in very many cases it can be proven that malignant diseases, and especially the different forms of cancer, are local, and that it is only after a time that the constitution begins to suffer; in other words, that the toxæmia is the secondary, and the local manifestation is the primary cause, whereas we have been taught that there was a constitutional predisposition to cancerous disease, which had a tendency to render any little bruise result in some form of cancer. This is, however, uncertain as yet.

Epithelioma may assume a most sudden and rapid growth, and may so undermine the constitution that life may be in danger, and death result from what is termed vegetating epithelioma or cauliflower excrescence.

This case of epithelioma undoubtedly arises from smoking a clay pipe. The pipe becomes very hot, dries away the tissues, and so a tendency to the disease is produced. It generally begins as a hard pimple under the skin—a hard nodule under the skin—which gradually comes nearer the surface, and is accompanied by peculiar stinging or burning pains, but not so much burning as we find in the true varieties of cancer. Finally, it ulcerates, and the ulceration is peculiar, consisting of elevated papillæ.

I think that, with the exception of the head of the penis, there is no more sensitive structure of the human body, than is the lip. I am now going to cut out the side of this lip, and the question is, what structures do I expect to go through. The lips are formed of mucus membrane, and chiefly of the muscle called the orbicularis oris, to which muscle is attached a great many other muscles. For instance we have the anguli oris, the levator menti, the zygomatic major and zygomatic minor, the buccinator or trumpeter's muscle. These are all more or less blended with the orbicularis oris, and all assist in the free play of the lips, moving them in many ways. By the lips we mould speech; we use wind instruments, we talk, we sing. They perform various functions. If it were not for the lips we would never be able to give sweet kisses —and that is a very important function—necessary sometimes to be performed, but always better in private than in public; be, sure, however, that you have a proper subject to operate upon.

We have also in the lips the coronary arteries, which are branches of the facial. The facial artery comes up in this direction, crosses diagonally and divides into two—the superior and inferior coronary; and it is this inferior coronary artery which will be cut across in this operation.

In removing epithelioma, it is very necessary that you cut out enough of the structure; and it is really quite remarkable how much can be removed, and how good an operation can be made by taking out a large quantity of the lip. Those who were here at the last year's clinics will recollect that nearly the whole of the chin was taken off at one operation. I expect a patient here to-day from whom I removed the whole integument of the chin in extirpating a large mark which the girl had since her birth. Her mother was frightened by seeing a mouse, and when she was born she had on her chin an oblong, black spot, full of hairs, which resembled exactly the back of a mouse. It was taken out, leaving the vermillion border of the lip intact. It extended around the chin and covered so much of the surface that when the lips of the wound were drawn together the centre of the lips almost touched the nose; but nature has behaved so well to the surrounding structures that the lip has come down in such a manner that you can now scarcely see any deformity.

Here is a specimen showing the position of the muscles we shall have to cut through. Here you see the orbicularis oris, the zygomatic major and minor, the labii inferiororis and the angali oris muscles; and here you see the arteries—the facial coming up on this side, winding around the jaw and dividing into the superior and inferior coronary.

The first incision that I shall make in this case is the one nearest the medial line. There is a good deal of hemorrhage about this operation. You see how the artery spurts. I will now make an incision directly down in this way. These arteries do not generally require ligation. If you do not twist them the bleeding ceases when the cut surfaces are approximated. You can make very nice, clean work of this. It is important that these sutures should be taken down very deep. I shall take the stitch nearly a quarter of an inch back, and bring it out like *that.* Then draw up the lip as nearly as you can.

We will now apply one part of calendula to four of water. Keep it on for about two days, and remove the lint the second or third day. There is a good deal to be said about the removal of these pins. The time at which they should be removed varies greatly. If you leave them until suppuration is noticed around the heads, you may be sure that you will have a mark afterwards, which about the face is always disagreeable, especially to a young lady. Therefore, on the morning of the third day you should try the pins by rotating them, and if you perceive that they are a little loose, do not wait for a drop of pus to be noticed, but cut the thread—don't untwist it—and then remove the pin by a rotary motion. It used to be the notion that in a suture one continuous thread should be used; but I have found that in using a continuous thread you obstruct the circulation a good deal between the pins, and that it is better to take a single piece for each pin, and not to extend the thread from one to the other.

The next case is

Angular Curvature of the Spine.

CECILIA FITZGERALD, *Aged Four Years.*

The mother states that the child has never been healthy; that she had the whooping cough during the summer and the measles in January. That during the spring and summer she has had a pain and cramp in her hip.

Here is the beginning of a disease which will result in deformity unless some remedy can be applied. You know the position of the spinal column, and that it is the axis which supports the trunk, and that it is made for its support. You know that it has four distinct curves or arches, in order that it may the better support the structure. When you examine the spinal column *per se*, when you recollect the number of bones that enter into its construction, and the variety of processes which come from these bones, as well as the wonderful motion which is permitted to the different parts of the spinal column, you cannot but be struck with amazement at the beauty of its mechanism, especially when you think of the motions of which it is capable, combined with its immense strength. On each side of the column we have certain varieties of muscles which should be symmetrical; they are attached to the processes of the column; and when these muscles act conjointly equilibrium is maintained. If, on the other hand, there is an antagonism between these muscles—if one set of them seems to have a tendency to draw the column to one side, then we have as the result, a lateral curvature of the spine. If the disease attacks the bodies of the vertebræ, and extends itself to the intervertebral substance, then there is a tendency in the front part of the vertebra to drop down, and the spinous processes push directly backward. This deformity is called Potts' disease of the spine, or, angular curvature of the spine. It arises chiefly from a carious condition of the bodies of the vertebræ, wherever you find it, and is accompanied in a great many instances by disorder of digestion. We find it chiefly in children having light hair and blue eyes, and a tendency to an enlargement of the glands—in other words, in scrofulous children generally.

On looking at the back of this child, as you now see it, you would scarcely detect anything out of the way, but if you take a profile view of it you can plainly detect the curvature.

The mother states that when the child was seven or eight months old she fell down some steps, and ever since that time has had a tendency to carry her head sideways.

There is one peculiarity about angular curvature of the spine which I wish to mention; it is, that in the majority of instances you can trace it to some injury received in years gone by, but that if the child grows, and the general health is sustained, the disease is likely to be cured, leaving, however, some deformity.

The object of the splint which I now apply is to lift the weight from the superincumbent part—from the sore, inflamed, irritable vertebræ. There are two pads attached to it, which make a pressure on each side of the column. This splint must be worn night and day.

The next case is

Cicatrices.

SUSAN CHRINE, *Aged Seven.*

(The mother states that nearly seven years ago the child was burned on the cheek by the side of the eye).

This is a very peculiar case. This sore has for some time been suppurating and discharging, occasionally healing over and then gathering again. There are certain varieties of inflammatory action which seem to undermine the tissues from place to place—in fact, to have a disposition to spread by reason of contiguity of surface. Here was an unhealthy action which began with a burn. Inflammatory action went on in one direction and the process of repair went on with it in another. Inflammation covers not only the process of repair, but it covers the process of disintegration, and even the death of the part. At the same time that the pus is forming, there may be a reparative process going on in the same structure. We find this same thing in that variety of ulcers which are called serpiginous ulcers. They seem to extend in a circle, and as fast as one part heals another is destroyed. Now, the question is, what is the best remedy to apply?

(The mother states that the child has taken no medicine).

There is no medicine that acts on cicatrices so well as silicea. Wherever and whenever, under any circumstances, you can apply the appropriate homœopathic medicines for surgical disease and cure your patient according to the homœopathic law, it is better than operative interference; true, it does not make such a brilliant appearance but it is better surgery, and it redounds more to the credit of the school than using the knife.

Give this remedy of the 30th dilution three times per day.

Surgical Clinic of October 24.

Before the patients were introduced to the class, Prof. Helmuth having the week previous been lecturing upon the inflammatory process and its terminations, began the lecture as follows:

Ulceration is that process by which a solution of continuity is effected in a living solid; it is of much more frequent occurrence in the cellular and adipose tissue than in muscles, tendons, ligaments, nerves or blood vessels.

Formerly the Hunterian theory was generally received that such breach of continuity was effected by what was termed ulcerative absorption, or, in other words, that the absorbent vessels were chiefly concerned in the establishment of the process; modern pathologists regard ulceration as the molecular death of a part—a gradual softening and disintegration of tissue, molecule by molecule; the effete matter being mixed with purulent and other secretions, and thus carried out of the system. This process is generally a sequel to true inflammation, or connected in some degree with inflammatory action.

If the inflammatory process continues, suppuration, softening, disintegration and detachment of the tissues in minute portions follow in succession the abnormal action; the separated molecules become mixed with the pus, and are removed with the discharge. Ulceration is the medium between suppuration and gangrene.

ULCERS are those sores that are produced by the ulcerative process, or, in other words, solutions of continuity in any of the soft parts of the body discharging purulent matter, found principally on the natural surfaces of the body, and originating frequently in a constitutional disorder. A sore discharging pus effected by ulceration is termed an *ulcer*.

Now, merely to show you, gentlemen, how some cases in our practice are criticized, I will relate the following to you:

On the 1st day of November, 1872, a sea captain aged sixty-five years, who had had scurvy, and who had been taking mercury, and who had visited many ports, was getting over a fence, and struck his shin; a black and blue spot made its appearance, which continued to increase, this he doctored himself, putting on a little hot and cold water. On the 12th day of November he sent for Dr. H., who is a physician, seventy-two years of age, and has been practicing homœopathy for twenty-five years and allopathy for the same time. He immediately told him that he thought it was a constitutional sore, and to adopt constitutional treatment, and to apply arnica and water. For ten days, up to the 22d of November, the sore became worse, the black and blue spot began to suppurate and to bleed. Around and about the bottom of the ulcer three, or four, or five vesicles made their appearance. Then the doctor made a solution of nitrate of silver (he had practiced a good deal in the country, and he always carried a stick in his pocket); applied it around the sore and upon its surface; it pained a great deal when the solution was applied. The ulceration then appeared to be stationary, the slough was apparently separating from the centre, and a yellowish pus was being discharged. But the patient became dissatisfied, and, through some outside influence, called in another surgeon. About the 1st day of January this other surgeon called, and what he did I don't know; I know the ulcer was discharging around the edges, and carbolic acid was applied, and the secretion was immediately arrested; the sore grew worse, and went on enlarging from the 1st of September to the 7th day of April, when the leg was amputated above the knee. The patient then sues Dr. H. for ten thousand dollars damages; stating that it was the application of the nitrate of silver that brought about the condition which resulted in amputation of the leg. All manner of questions were put to me on my cross-examination, many of them foolish in the extreme, and having no bearing whatever upon the case, which, however, terminated favorably for our side.

Q. What is inflammation?

A. Inflammation, when fully established, consists in an engorgement of the capillary vessels, dependent on their diminished action, and the relaxed condition of their coats, together with more or less accelerated motion of the heart and arteries. From such an abnormal condition arise the well known characteristic symptoms—pain, heat, swelling and redness. (Dolor, calor, tumor, rubor.)

Q. What is congestion?

A. Congestion is the preternatural increase of blood in the capillary vessels, or excessive local fulness of the small blood vessels—an unnatural accumulation of blood in any part of the body, or any subordinate system.

Q. What is suppuration?

A. Suppuration is a pure process of luxuriation, by means of which superfluous parts are produced, which do not acquire that degree of consolidation, or permanent connection with one another, and with the neighboring parts which is necessary for the existence of the body. Pus is not the dissolving, but the dissolved, *i. e.*, transformed tissue. A part becomes soft and liquifies while suppurating, but it is not the pus which occasions this softening, on the contrary, it is the pus which is produced as the result of the proliferation of the tissues.

Q. Suppose a part to be suppurating, and something is applied to that part which suddenly checks the formation of pus, is that a good or bad sign? Bad; it drives the pus into the blood. Any sudden check of suppuration, set it down as a rule, is bad.

Traumatic Paralysis.

PETER CARTER, *Aged Twenty-four.*

This man fell and injured the musculo-spiral nerve, so he has no use of his arm.

Q. Have you applied electricity? A. Yes.

Q. How many times have you taken electricity? A. Three times a week.

Q. For how long a time? A. From ten minutes to a quarter of an hour.

Q. Did you have any feeling as the current passed down the arm? A. Yes, sir.

Q. Do you feel it any more now than you did when it was first applied? A. Yes.

Q. Do you have any numbness in your hands? Yes, sir.

Q. Does that sensation of numbness increase or diminish? A. It is about the same.

Q. Are you sensitive to the cold—can you feel cold and heat? A. Yes, sir.

The sensory nerves appear all right; he has a good appetite. He has been taking Rhus Toxicodendron three times a day This man has also a large red spot on his left leg. There appears to be fluctuation in the tissue, but whether there is pus in it, or whether it is serum, it is pretty hard to detect. I have a notion it is serum. I believe that should the parts be opened with an incision, probably it would be a long time before the wound would heal. He should be allowed to keep himself quiet, and elevate the foot and keep it bandaged. The idea is to prevent local congestion. The part may be either strapped or it may be bandaged. I think I will strap it; I will show you how to strap a sore. In applying plaster it is always necessary that it should be put on as smoothly as possible, and that each strap of plaster should be drawn uniformly tight; if you put on one strap tolerably tight, and the next one a little tighter, the one below loses its efficacy—it ruffs up. Now, this strapping is very excellent treatment in certain classes of indolent ulcer where the limb needs a great deal of support; it equalizes the circulation. In the first place, let me tell you about straps. In order to put straps on properly you must have the part shaved. You saw me try to put some straps upon a man who had his beard on, and the result was that there was no support to the part, and the wound separated. Where there is bristly hair, such as you have on the recently shaved chin, the straps stick like the mischief, and give a great deal of pain when removed. In the first place, to cover that sore it must be perfectly dry. I will take the strap *this* way and let it go all the way over. I then reverse the manner of application and begin on the other side, allowing one strap to cross the other at the centre of the sore. The idea is to put them on alternately and make them come in a line.

Scirrhus.

BRIDGET MCNALLY.

This woman came to us with a cancer in her breast, and I cut it out. She had it removed with the expectation of getting married. To the patient:

Q. Did you go and do it? A. No, sir.

Q. You have been a great deal better, haven't you, Jane? A. Yes, sir.

That wound looks very well; there is no indication of a return of the disease. From appearances I should suppose that there is a tendency to abscess, and I think that Hepar would be a very excellent medicine. I will give it to her in the 30th dilution.

She looked in a most miserable condition when she came here, now she seems to be getting better. She has an axillary abscess and a severe cold.

Q. Can you put your hand to your head? A. Yes, sir.

Q. Good appetite? A. Yes, sir.

Q. You were very fond of a little drink once in a while, were you not? A. Oh, very fond, indeed.

Fracture of the Humerus.

JOHN A. POWERS.

JOHN A. POWERS, see page 9, arm. It has been two weeks to-day since he was here. Now let me see the other hand, one is about as dirty as the other. I will move his hand; now put it out straight again; touch your head with it; now turn it over this way, now back. There is nothing so grateful to a patient with a broken arm as good bathing after taking the bandages off. The arm is doing well.

Necrosis of Frontal Bone.

ROBERT DAILY, *Aged Twenty-five.*

Q. What is your name? A. Robert Daily.

Q. How old are you? A. Twenty-five years old.

This is an affection of the forehead, which has been troublesome since April, and was caused by being kicked by a horse. A Dr. Moore opened it.

Q. Did any spiculæ of bone come out? A. No, sir.

Q. Have you been anywhere else for treatment? A. No, sir.

There is a peculiar appearance about a wound from which a piece of bone comes out, or where there is a sequestrum; the parts are puckered; seems to protrude. The appearance is like an unhealthy granulation, and there is puckering around it. This bone is exposed, I can feel it distinctly; but it is not loose, there appears to be a small piece of bone that wants to come out. (To the patient.) I will pull that out for you.

Necrosis bears the same relation to the osseous system that mortification does to the soft parts. Caries is an ulceration; Necrosis is the death of the bone. What is the difference between ulceration and mortification? The difference between ulceration and mortification is this—that in the ulcerative process there is no regular death *en masse*, but in mortification there is. It is astonishing how small a piece of diseased bone will give rise to extensive suppuration; a small piece of bone underneath the skin may give rise to a great deal of inflammatory action. I shall take hold of that bone once more; I think it is not large, but it is fast. I find that is firmly attached. It would be a wrong process to take a larger pair of forceps and remove it. You must go home and have the part poulticed. I will give him silicea 30th, which he will take three times a day, and I think that by next Saturday the bone will be loose, and can be removed. Until the bone comes away there will be no use in attempting to cure the wound. I pull it with all my might, but it does not move. He is to use simply a bread and milk poultice.

Epithelioma.

PATRICK MURPHY, *Aged Eighty-five.*

(*Continued from page* 19.)

You all saw on Monday afternoon this patient was in a most excellent condition, and the reason that I removed the pins on this day, which is rather sooner than it is usually done, was because there was beginning suppuration about the pins, and the threads were beginning to cut through. Whenever that happens, it is always a rule to extract the pins. We put on a strap, but that did not hold, because he had not been shaved. Then Dr. Boynton and others in charge of it applied silver sutures. Here is a man eighty-five years of age, and he comes here and has his cancer cut out because he wants to live. Life is sweet to all of us.

Q. Do you feel better? A. Yes, sir.

Q. How old are you now? A. 85 years.

Q. Where were you born? A. In Ireland.

Hypertrophy of Tonsils.

A. H. B., *Aged Nineteen.*

Q. What is your name? A. H. B.

Q. How old are you? A. Nineteen.

This young gentleman has had, since he was eight years old, Tonsillitis, or Cynanche Tonsillaris.

This term denotes an inflammatory affection of the fauces, chiefly resident in and around the tonsils. It is ordinarily the result of atmospheric exposure, and is characterized by swelling and redness of the back part of the throat, accompanied with difficulty of swallowing, impeded respiration, difficult articulation, marked alteration of the voice, fever and other ordinary constitutional accompaniments, according to the intensity of the inflammatory action. In the acute form suppuration often results, and we have Quinsy. In other instances, as the present, the disease is chronic, and the tonsils remain enlarged.

Q. Have you done much for this affection? A. Yes, sir.

Q. Taken a good deal of medicine? A. Yes, sir.

Q. Do you know what medicines you have taken, or who has prescribed for you? A. My father.

Q. He is a physician? A. Yes, sir.

You have taken, perhaps, all the homœopathic remedies, and it is a question now, what shall we do in the case? Here is a gentleman who has been under the treatment of a skilful physician, and still he is no better.

The tonsils (tonsillæ, amygdalæ) are two prominent bodies, which occupy the recesses formed, one on each side of the fauces, between the anterior and posterior palatine arches.

They are usually about eight lines in length, and four in width and thickness, but they vary much in size in different individuals.

The outer side of the tonsil is connected with the inner surface of the superior constrictor of the pharynx, and approaches very near to the internal carotid artery. Its inner surface, projecting into the fauces between the palatine arches, presents from twelve to fifteen orifices, which give it a perforated appearance. These orifices lead into recesses in the substance of the tonsil, from which other and smaller orifices conduct still deeper into numerous compound crypts or follicles, the whole being lined with continuations of the buccal mucous membrane. The tonsils, therefore, consist of groups of compound muciparous crypts. They yield a mucous fluid which lubricates the fauces. The tonsils receive a very large supply of blood from many sources, viz., from the tonsillar and palatine branches of the facial artery, and from the descending palatine, the ascending pharyngeal, and the dorsalis linguæ. The veins are numerous, and enter the tonsillar plexus on its outer side. Its nerves come from the glosso pharyngeal nerve, and from the fifth pair.

Q. What are the fauces?

A. The posterior part of the mouth terminated by the pharynx and larynx.

To the patient:

Q. Do you snore at night? A. Yes.

Q. Pretty loud sometimes? A. Yes, sir.

Q. Your mouth is very dry in the morning? A. Yes.

Q. You have some sensation of choking in your throat? A. Yes, sir.

Whenever he becomes cold there is an increase of saliva and difficulty of breathing. What should we do with this boy? If he did not have to attend our lectures I would immediately cut out these tonsils; under the present circumstances I should think he had better take merc. sol. 3d three times a day, and just before the holidays at Christmas times we will shave off the ends of the tonsils. He has been taking potash. There are a variety of medicines which are used with success in hypertrophy of the tonsils. The preparations of mercury and potash, of course; baryta., calc. carb., sulph., silic., lach., hepar., and others. But there is, also, a treatment for the removal of large tonsils without the knife, which has been very successfully employed in London, and which is simple and efficacious, in that it does not confine the patient to the house. It is the application of the so-called London paste, prepared of equal parts of caustic soda and lime, moistened with a little alcohol. It must be kept in a well-stoppered bottle, since caustic soda and lime have a powerful affinity for carbonic acid. If exposed, therefore, to the air the causticity of the paste is lost. Various tests have also satisfied me that it is necessary to employ absolute alcohol in preparing it.

In practice I proceed as follows: A quantity of equal parts of finely pulverized and well mixed caustic soda and unslacked lime is kept on hand. When an application is to be made to the tonsils, a little of the powder is put into a small porcelain cup, a few drops of absolute alcohol, which is kept near at hand, are added, the two are carefully mixed with a glass rod, when the paste is ready for use. The patient must be placed in a good light, a tongue depressor used, and the paste applied and allowed to remain for several seconds, until an eschar be produced. Then the paste is washed off and the parts allowed to slough, when the paste must again be applied. Care must be taken that the paste is applied only to affected parts. It is likely, if too much is placed upon the rod, that some of it will drop off, which causes great excoriation.

Dr. Morrell Mackenzie, of London, reports 200 cases in his own practice which he has absolutely cured. I think we will apply this preparation to this patient about once every three days.

Note.—The treatment was carried on for some time; and during the vacation at Christmas the outside of each tonsil was shaved off—a perfect recovery followed.

Indolent Ulcer.

JANE R. S., *Aged* 38.

There have been many classifications of ulcers attempted from time to time, and I think these may be simplified by dividing them into the simple, the indolent and the irritable ulcer. In the latter we generally have the symptoms which indicate a vitiated state of the constitution and disorders of digestion. We find the irritable sore in the upper ranks of society, among high livers, club men, men who dine out as a business, drink a great deal of wine and eat highly seasoned food. The edges of this sore are jagged, undermined and serrated. The face of the ulcer is uneven and worm-eaten, the discharge is unhealthy, thin and sanious, the granulations are flabby and bleed easily, the blood being of a dark grumous color.

The medicines that have proved most effectual in removing this form of ulcer are arsen., asaf., carbo-veg., lyc., hepar, merc.-sol., nit.-acid, silic., mez., con., sulph., thuja, staphys.

Gentlemen, look at this sore. You perceive the edges are elevated and smooth, not serrated, as in the form I have just shown you. You see that the surface is smooth, there are no granulations and that the color is tawny and gray. You perceive also that the margins are callous (this one especially so), and appear like a ring of cartilage. This is called by some authors "the callous ulcer." You see also the condition of this patient—she is poor, and bears with her those characteristic marks of poverty which are too well known to us. If this patient could have her method of life changed, an immediate improvement would result.

Q. Could you come into our hospital? A. No, sir.

Q. Why not? A. I have to work, sir.

Q. Have you a large family? A. Yes, sir, small children.

Q. Could you keep your leg elevated in a chair, or could you go to bed for ten days or so? A. No, sir; the times are too hard.

You see, gentlemen, it is as I have anticipated; so, under these circumstances, we must do the best for her that we can. Before, however, I proceed with the treatment, let me say that you must not confound a scrofulous ulcer with the sloughing ulcer, which is more like what is termed "hospital gangrene." An indolent ulcer is an ulcer with irregular overhanging edges, with little pus with unhealthy granulations presenting around the edges of the sore, which extends into the surrounding texture. If you put your probe into the face of an indolent ulcer you will find the parts are callous, and the extreme frequency of this callosity has given rise to the term "callous ulcer." An indolent ulcer in a depraved constitution and on the lower extremities, where we have nine tenths of them, is very difficult indeed to manage; not so much on account of the position of the ulcer, but generally on account of the constitutional diseases which exist in the system. The sore is merely a manifestation of this constitutional weakness, and, therefore, it is very important, if you expect to cure radically an indolent ulcer, to adopt strictly constitutional measures. As a general rule, indeed you may set it down as a law, that grease of all kinds interferes with the curative process; therefore ointments are bad for ulcers.

In very many patients we have a condition of ulcer which is termed varicose. Such an ulcer is nothing more nor less than an indolent ulcer. Sometimes an irritation takes place in a vein, it opens, and a certain amount of hemorrhage results therefrom; the edges of the sore are overhanging and purple, they become somewhat callous, and not at all sensitive to the touch, and this condition is termed a varicose ulcer. The supply of blood having been cut off, the other veins attempt to do the work that should be done by this vein, and they also enlarge, or there may be other obstruction to venous return. The method of cure for such ulcers is to release the local congestions by destroying the varicose conditions of the part. Now, you must understand me, that when we speak of these ulcers I do not include in this classification the so-called *specific* ulcers, but, nevertheless, will mention here a particular kind of sore, which is rather rare. It is similar to an indolent ulcer in a patient who has had scurvy. From the history of the cases which were observed in Dreadnaught Hospital, this ulcer begins with a black and blue spot under the cuticle from some external injury, which causes extravasation. After a certain number of days a redness appears around the edges of the spot, and a dark red substance in the centre begins to raise up, underneath which an unhealthy suppuration is noticed.

In the first place, to treat properly an indolent ulcer, if it is a possible thing, we want to support the part; it must be elevated, and should be thoroughly cleansed; cleanliness is almost indispensable in the treatment of this form of ulcer, and the best way in which it can be cleansed is by carbolic acid spray, one part of carbolic acid to 100 water. Then the limb should be supported with a roller, and the more the patient can be left on the back the better. For ulcers—old ulcers, where the parts are blue and overhanging—the best medicine is *arsenicum*, and the next best is *carbo veg.* With the proper applications you can cure these ulcers, provided the patient will always do as you direct.

The reason ulcers are so difficult to cure is, because the patients are generally of the lower classes of men or women, who have to work for their living and are obliged to be on their feet; or else the refugees of society, who care for nothing except their whiskey, and wander about the streets in a most pitiable condition.

There are a great many local methods of treatment for ulcers, which I shall mention at the next lecture. We have electricity, we have the earth treatment of Hewson, and a great many other methods, all of which I hope to be able to give you at the next lecture, or as the cases present themselves at the clinics.

What is scurvy? Scurvy is that condition of the system, or a depraved condition of the blood, in which there is a tendency to fibrinous exudations in different parts of the body. At the same time there is a tendency to suppuration, ulceration and œdema, either in the gums or about the bones or different portions of the body; the system suffers severely and the cure of the disease is brought about chiefly by giving the patient acids and vegetable diet, such as potatoes. You will find it principally among people who have not had a sufficient supply of vegetable food and acids, and who have lived on salt beef and salt pork. On board ships acids are generally provided to prevent the crew from having the scurvy.

Mother's Mark.

Dr. Helmuth (holding up a piece of flesh and hair in a bottle) said: There is the skin of a patient's chin; this was a mother's mark. This girl's mother was four or five months gone in pregnancy, and was very much frightened by seeing a mouse; when the child was born, on the chin was this thing, covered with hair, and very dark hair it was. If you look at it sideways you will see it looks exactly like a mouse without a tail. The hair has turned white from being in alcohol, but it was perfectly dark when the growth was removed. The question arises, can the nervous influence of the mother be transmitted to a child? I am just as certain that it can as I am that I am here. I know of a patient who was frightened with seeing a case of small pox, and her child was born with pustules on it.

Surgical Clinic of October 31st, 1874.

The first case to-day is that of Patrick Murphy, who was operated on two weeks ago for epitheloma of the lip. You will recollect that on the Monday following my last clinic the pins were withdrawn. It was rather an early day, but the union seemed so complete that I thought it advisable to withdraw the pins, and ordered adhesive straps applied. He was taken at night with a severe fit of coughing, which tore open the parts, and it was necessary to replace the pins. Last Saturday he was here, and other sutures used, but they came out. He came back on Tuesday, Dr. Thompson pared the edges afresh and applied new sutures, which are now to be removed.

You will recollect how perfect the union seemed when those pins were removed on the third day. Of course, after the sutures have torn out, we have to be extremely careful. In plastic operations like this, and in the operation for hare lip, the silk is oftentimes left after removing the pins, thereby affording considerable support. I have now removed the three pins, and the silk suture in the vermilion border of the lip. I should have taken the precaution to have had this man shaved, but now it is too late as the traction of the skin by shaving might break away the uniting points, I shall therefore leave his beard as it is, as it is now four or five days since he was shaved.

I will now paint collodion upon the plaster. Very often after operations of this kind, and after that for hare lip, even after the parts have become almost perfectly united, I have known them torn apart by sneezing or coughing. Therefore, I usually take care, in operations of this kind in children, to paint the whole surface over with collodion. There are compressors which draw the parts together and take off the traction. In some instances incisions on the side are made to prevent the strain.

Subclavian Aneurism.

JOHN R. JONES, *Aged* 40.

This patient comes from Poultney, Vermont.

When you examine a patient you must always do so carefully and thoroughly. The greatest error that I ever made in my life in a surgical diagnosis was because I made it in a hurry. When I enter upon fractures and dislocations I will tell you of the mistake that I made—since which time, I assure you, I have been more careful, and have taken more time for my examinations.

There is an epidemic in suicides sometimes, and there are epidemics often in labor cases. Sometimes there seem to be epidemics in deaths. I have not had an aneurism to treat for a considerable time, and now I have four on hand.

We will get this man's history, and that as accurately as possible; and, if I do not mistake, this will prove a very interesting case.

If you listen, with your ear at the root of the neck on the right side, you will not only hear pulsation, but you will hear a puffing sound, which is called the *bruit.* That is the peculiar puffing sound that you have in an aneurism.

An aneurism is an enlargement of an artery in some part of its course, the cavity of which communicates with the long diameter of the vessel. In other words, an aneurism is an enlargement of an artery—either spherical or longitudinal—and presents peculiar and unmistakable signs, such as the pulsation, which pulsation is simultaneous with the beats of the heart and also *bruit.* We have a variety of aneurism, in which only one side of the tube is enlarged; and we have a fusiform aneurism, in which the whole circumference of the artery seems to be involved. As a general rule, however, it is only one side of the vessel which is dilated, and we detect in it the symptoms of pulsation simultaneous with the beats of the heart, and the bruit, or puffing sound which you have heard.

Aneurisms, as a general rule, begin suddenly, and often result from some sudden shock or strain. A person may be predisposed to them by certain diseases incident to the arterial coats, as atheroma, which is a softening or deterioration of the internal coats of the artery.

The patient states that his attention was first called to the swelling last August; that he has not had any difficulty in breathing, although he has noticed an occasional accumulation of phlegm in the throat, and that his voice has become more husky than formerly; he had been working with a derrick, but does not recollect that he had been straining himself more than usual, but woke up in the morning and found a small lump, which pained him somewhat; he has experienced no difficulty in swallowing; but had slight cough.

In the formation of aneurisms we always find what are called the active and the passive clot. As the blood is impelled through the aneurism by the beats of the heart, there is an effusion of fibrine which takes place around the circumference of the aneurismal sac, and this becoming partially organized forms itself into strata, becomes of the color of currant jelly, and is termed the *active clot.* In aneurisms about the aorta this clot sometimes becomes so large that the pulsation is almost indiscernable. Then, through the centre of this active clot, we have what is called the passive clot, or a clot which is thinner, and which allows the blood to pass through into the circulation.

One of the methods of cure suggested by Sir William Fergusson is that of manipulation, in which this active clot is brokén in pieces, and forced by the current into the channel of the artery.

The subject of aneurism is possèssed of so much importance, covers so wide a field in surgical literature, and has interested the minds of so many surgeons throughout the world, from a remote period to the present, that I propose to take up the subject in my next daily lecture (without waiting to arrive at diseases of the arteries in regular order), and, with this case before you, to lecture upon the subject of aneurism, properly so called. Then we will suggest the means of relief we think proper, after due consultation. Several different methods have been proposed, and many of them followed with success; but it requires a great deal of judgment and thought—taking all the items of the case into consideration—to determine which method shall be adopted. I am glad to be able to bring this patient before you, because he seems wiliing and able to follow up the necessary treatment, and you shall see the result.

Potts', or Angular Curvature of the Spine.

At the last clinic but one I showed you a case of Potts' disease of the spine almost in its incipiency. This is a case very much developed. In the other case the disease was lower down the spine; here we have it in the dorsal vertebra. It is not necessary for me to add anything by way of description of Potts' disease of the spine. I simply need to say that there are certain medicines which act internally, according to the homœopathic principle, which have a tendency to arrest the disease of the bone which is going on. Mechanical treatment, in this variety of disease—whether it is Potts' disease of the spine, or curvature of the spine laterally, or disease of the hip—is always of great avail—of as much service as a splint, in a case of fracture; but there, also, are certain internal medicines which, if properly administered and persevered in for a length of time, will be of decided benefit. I have known Potts' disease of the spine arrested in its incipiency without the use of a brace, in cases where you could keep the patient prone in the horizontal position. But the trouble is, that a majority of the patients who suffer from Potts' disease are scrofulous children. This is an exception, I think. It is this very vitiated condition of the constitution which is so admirably relieved and cured by the proper internal administration of medicine. Therefore, while you should as surgeons look into and understand all the recent improvements which belong to the mechanical appliances in surgery, it is just as important, and even more so, that you should understand the application of those medicines which, properly administered, will eradicate *the predisposition* upon which this disorder depends.

The splint on this patient is a much better one than that which I showed you on the last case of Potts' disease. The object is to support the upper part of the trunk and keep the weight from resting on the diseased vertebra. The internal administration of medicine is of great importance. In the investigation we have to be guided as much by constitutional peculiarities, by the looks of the child, by the previous history of the parents, and other objective symptoms, as by the result of any minute inquiries with reference to the increase or diminution of the symptoms, which the patient, because of youth, may be unable to answer. There are some medicines, such as petroleum, phosphate of lime, phosphorus, iodine, calcarea-carb., sulphur, mezerium, which may be used to advantage, but I have seen more good results from the use of phosphate of lime, and from mezerium, than any other two of the medicines I have mentioned. But do not understand me to say that these medicines are specifics for every case, because I do not. In these clinics I can only give you the names of the medicines from which you may select the special remedy applicable to a particular case. Therefore, I say that in a majority of cases I have found the phosphate of lime and mezerium useful. In these cases the periosteum seems to be disordered rather than the bone itself; but when there is a good deal of pain, and symptoms of fever set in, and the restlessness which follows any irritation of the system, you will soon discover the peculiar condition of the pulse which indicates an irritative fever. An irritative fever may be occasioned by any irritation going on in the system, from any occult cause. The patient wastes away, sweats, is pale, loses appetite, is fretful, peevish, the pulse stands at 120; he does not sleep at night and is depressed in mind. Whether it is a disease in the hip, or in the spine, or some other portion of the body, the symptoms point to an irritation in the system, which often begins in the first stages of Potts' disease, and before any local manifestation is looked for. Therefore it is that in these obscure cases, when you find an irritative fever, that the most careful examination be made in order that you may arrive at a correct diagnosis. Never be in a hurry to give a diagnosis. It is always a great deal better to wait, and especially never to put your ideas on paper until you are sure you are right. Many men have got themselves into a scrape by haste. When you are *sure*, then you may sign your name, but don't do it if there is a loophole by which somebody else can get hold of you and throw your diagnosis over. A man of inferior perception makes a good diagnosis in the advanced stage of the disease, and may thus, perhaps, outshine a more scientific or highly educated man who has seen the patient in the earlier stages of the same affection. Many a physician and many a surgeon has attended a patient straight through all the primary symptoms of disease, and has examined and studied up the case, yet could not tell exactly what was the matter, until the patient becomes dissatisfied; and, perhaps, just as the disease develops itself, another doctor is called in, and receives all the benefit of the diagnosis, because the symptoms are more perceptible to the senses. These are some of the injustices that may be done to the surgeon or physician. Therefore, I say that when you find an irritating fever, or symptoms indicating a certain amount of fever in the system, be careful how you make your diagnosis. A mistake in surgery is unfortunate. A mistake in medicine is frequently never known. The difference is this: the doctor attends a patient, makes a mistake, and the patient dies; he has been attended for the wrong disease, but he dies and nobody is the wiser. A surgeon makes a mistake—makes a crooked arm, perhaps, which is held up before a jury for his damnation, and the result is that thousands of dollars are claimed for the mistake. Death covers a doctor's errors, but a surgeon's are held up before an illiterate jury. These suits for malpractice are beautiful! I do not know of anything that makes a man sleep sounder at night than a suit for malpractice.

Lateral Spinal Curvature.

NEWMAN MEYER, 11 *Years Old.*

The father states: "About a year ago I noticed that this boy did not play as usual. A little later he would wake up at night and come down stairs, saying that he could not sleep. Then we took him to Morrisville and had him examined by a physician. The doctor said that he had the "sciatica," and blistered him on his back, near the hips. A little later we employed two physicians. They still called it sciatica, and cupped his back, and gave him medicines of various kinds. Then they changed their opinion, and called it "spinal irritation." The boy got worse, and then we had a doctor by the name of Kelly, who introduced himself to me, and said that he was sent to me by my brother-in-law. He said that there were no symptoms of spinal irritation, but that it was a perfect case of sciatica. We then went to doctoring him again for sciatica, but without any good results. Then that doctor left him, and I didn't know what to do next. I noticed that when the doctors would stay away from me, and I attended him, that he would seem to be easier. About four weeks ago a doctor by the name of Waterbury, formerly from New York, asked permission to come over and mend up my boy. Said he, "I know more than all these doctors; I have had a good chance; I have been in the city, and I know all about it." Finally I consented to have him come. He examined the boy. That was the first time the boy had been stripped and examined. He had been examined only through his clothes before. The boy had, then, not walked for about ten weeks, but this doctor got him on his feet, and urged him to walk a little. After he examined him he said, "If old Dr. Sled was here he would call it 'worm palsy.'" Dr. Helmuth said, "I think the worms have not much to do with it, although they breed very fast in these cases." The patient continued: "He recommended an 'electrizing machine,' at first, and then he said that the boy would have to take opium continually and regularly. I did not like that, for I had about come to the conclusion not to give him any more preparations of opium, but he said that it would have to be done. Then he fixed up about a dozen pills, and put a little calomel in, so that they 'would not act upon the bowels.' I gave the pills to him that night, but the boy was worse. The following night I gave him the pills again, and still he seemed to be worse, and the same way with the next night. Then I went to see the doctor about it, and he told me to *give him an ounce of opium*—the clear stuff—the gum opium. By the time I got home my wife had given the boy three of those pills, and he was still groaning with the pain. The pain is more severe at night than in the day time, and he cries a great deal at night. I then gave him a chunk of opium about as big as a a pea, in addition to the pills he had already taken. I usually went to bed as soon as I got home at night, and would sleep till about midnight, while my wife took care of the boy, and then I would get up and take care of him until morning. While I was in bed my wife gave him three more morphine powders, and he was still crying when I got up. I took him, then, and he continued crying until daylight. My wife stated that she had also given him a double spoonful of paregoric to relieve his pain. He went to sleep about daylight, and slept all of that day and half of the next night. Then I said that that was the last opium he should take if he died for it."

Dr. Helmuth said: This is certainly an obscure case. You can see from that boy's expression of countenance how he has suffered; and you saw a moment ago, when I asked him to try to walk, what suffering the effort caused him. You must have respect for suffering whenever you see it; and when you see a human being writhing the way that poor child did, and at the same time endeavoring to conceal it, for your benefit, you ought to be thankful to him, as I am.

One of the peculiar characteristics of bone disease is the increase of pain at night.

From the examination I have made of this case I take it for granted that there must be some pressure upon the spinal cord. This is a very aggravated case of curvature of the spine, differing from the other cases that have been before us in the greater number of vertebra affected. If I mistake not this condition will go on until an abscess forms somewhere. The peculiarities of the pain that he has now, the loss of the power of motion, the pain of walking, the sufferings increasing at night—all seem to indicate a disease going on in the bony structure, and I believe in the spinal column, causing pressure upon the spinal cord, producing a certain amount of paralysis, and necessarily causing the patient great suffering and emaciation.

The question is, what can be done in such a case as this? I think that this boy can be benefited. In the first place he must have a proper apparatus, which shall take the weight off the hips as much as possible, and relieve the spinal column. I believe that if we could get the appropriate homœopathic medicine it would relieve him. I will give him *mezerium* and let you know the result I will give it in the 200th potency. Put one powder in a tumbler two thirds full of water, and give him a tablespoonful every two hours until this evening, and then, if the pain augments, give him a teaspoonful every fifteen or twenty minutes. In the meantime, I will try to have some appliance made which will have a tendency to take the pressure from the spinal cord, and prevent further deformity. With a proper appliance to take the pressure off the spine, we can, with the appropriate homœopathic medicine, greatly relieve the pain. There is no class of diseases in which medicines of the higher potency seem to act as well as in those of the nervous system.

Prolapsus Ani.

ELIZA THOMAS, 4 *Years Old.*

(The mother states that the child has been suffering from prolapsus ani, and that the bowels have been protruding for three or four weeks.) The patient was exposed on the table, and a mass of bluish black intestine, four inches long, was found between the nates.

It is wonderful that this bowel has not sloughed off before this. I do not know that I shall now be able to put it back as it should be done, but it must be returned pretty soon. The longer it is left out the worse the child will get. In reducing a prolapsed bowel you must do it gradually. With the fingers in *this* position, holding them as a cone, and lubricating them well, you push it up. (The bowel was then carefully returned.) When I get it in place I insert a sponge to hold it in position. It would be well to first soak the sponge in a strong solution of alum water, as that would have a tendency to make the bowels contract. I shall prescribe, as a medicine, *nux vomica.* I have had very excellent success attending its use in reducing prolapsed bowels. Administer *nux vomica* every two hours, and give only such articles of diet as will have a tendency to constipate the bowels. Give her chiefly boiled rice as food for the present.

Surgical Clinic of November 7th, 1874.

Subclavian Aneurism.

(Continued.)

Dr. Helmuth said: The patient we had here last Saturday is doing remarkably well. He returned on the following Monday, and upon a careful examination I find that he has a subclavian aneurism on the right side, I think in the second portion of the artery as it passes behind the scalenus anticus muscle. You all know the danger that is attendant upon aneurism of this artery, and you all understand the difficulties (or you will very soon, for I shall tell you) of its ligation. The subclavian artery has never been ligated successfully in the first part of its course on the right side, and on the left it is almost impracticable. The operation, I believe, has been performed only once, and then by J. Kearny Rogers, of the United States, some years ago. His patient did not survive. Taking into consideration the anatomical situation and the disastrous results that arise from cutting off so large a supply of blood, you will see what a hazardous, difficult and dangerous operation it is to tie the subclavian artery on either side in the first part of its course. In the second part of its course, on the right side, as it passes behind the scalenus anticus, it may be ligated, but it is difficult on account of the division of the muscle upon which lies the phrenic nerve, and also the close proximity of the internal jugular vein, a hemorrhage from which would almost certainly prove fatal. In the third part of its course the vessel may be tied, and the operations have been comparatively successful; I mean, perhaps 43 out of 100 have recovered. When I get further along in the treatment of aneurism I will give you the exact statistics.

These operations should never be undertaken, knowing how hazardous they are, until you have given the patient the benefit of every other known remedy. When a man takes an anæsthetic, and lies down on the table and surrenders himself to the surgeon's knife, to have one of these vessels ligated, it is almost like signing his death warrant. Therefore, I say, before any such risk is taken, it behooves us, as just men and good surgeons, to give him the benefit of all the knowledge we have in his case before we subject him to a difficult and hazardous operation.

The innominata has been tied, I think, about eleven times in all. To New York belongs the credit of having the first surgeon to tie this vessel. Valentine Mott was unsuccessful. I recollect reading an account of this case, and the intense interest that it presented to my mind. I remember the sentence in which, after describing how he had reached the innominata and the ligature was placed around the vessel, that he writes, "As I began tightening the ligature I never watched a human countenance with alternate feelings of fear and joy as I did that of the patient as I was drawing this ligature." He knew he was cutting off one-quarter the supply of the blood of the body, and he expected there would be great perturbation in the circulation, but such was not the case. Smyth, of New Orleans, has made the only successful ligature of the innominata, and he tied not only that vessel but the carotid, and checked the secondary hemorrhage, which came on from the subclavian, by means of small shot, which compressed the parts well. Hemorrhage, however, again recurring, the vertebral was tied and the patient recovered.

I have ordered this patient to be given five drops of veratrum viride every four hours. His pulse is about 110, and I desire it kept down to 65 or 68. What does that do? It does not cut off the supply of blood, but it depresses the action of the heart, it lessens the *vis a tergo*; it checks the flow into the artery and gives opportunity for a clot to form. If, instead of 110 strokes a minute, blood is forced into the vessel at the rate of 68 beats, you will see that there elapses between each beat a longer period, which affords time for the active clot to form. Besides this, I have ordered digital pressure of from five to eight minutes four or five times a day. It is perfectly unbearable at first; the patient lies over and seems to writhe in agony, yet I fancy the tumor is harder, and that it is not as sensitive as it was, and that he suffers less pain. But I am not deluded by these appearances, and am prepared for emergencies.

There are a great many other methods recommended for the cure of aneurism which it will be useless to try in this case. Suffice it to say, if, after having employed all the means in our power, the tumor increases, I will tie the subclavian; but that will not be resorted to until we are positive that every other means is exhausted.

This patient was removed to the hospital, and, after trying all means for relief without avail, Professor Helmuth tied the subclavian outside the scaleni. The endeavor was made to reach the innominata; but a second aneurism, at the root of the carotid, pressed laterally on the trachea and forward on the sternum, to such a degree, that access to the great trunk was impossible. The patient died of rupture of the sac, on its posterior surface, on the eighth day. He was rapidly improving in health. The excruciating pain had left his shoulder and arm, his pulse was fair, and temperature about 99.

The accompanying cut will show the double aneurism which existed in this case and the surrounding structures.

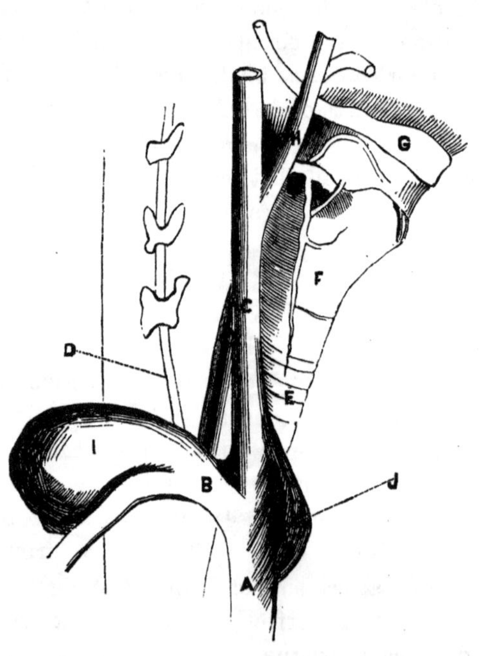

A—Innominata,	F—Larynx,
B—Subclavian,	G—Hyoid Bone,
C—Common Carotid,	H—External Carotid,
D—Vertebral,	I—Subclavian Aneurism,
E—Trachea,	J—Carotid Aneurism.

Phymosis.

A. X., *Aged Twenty-three Years.*

The first patient that I shall introduce to your notice this morning is a case of phymosis, and a very bad case, too.

Phymosis is congenital or acquired. Congenital phymosis is that variety in which at birth the prepuce is elongated. When it is acquired it comes from preternatural causes. This man stated to me that he had never been able to draw his prepuce backward any further than one-eighth of an inch (illustrating), and that lately he has had a very severe inflammation of the glans penis, and that then there was some discharge of fœtid matter, and that since he has been unable to draw back the fore-skin at all. Now, in order to prevent fresh inflammatory action and adhesion of the under surface of the prepuce and the upper surface of the glans, I propose to circumcise him this morning. I can simply slit the prepuce with the scissors; it is a very easy operation, but it does not make as nice a cure. A man does not enjoy the appearance of a slit prepuce. In this instance I shall cut off the projecting part of his fore-skin; you will find, then, that there will be an exposure of the mucous membrane. I shall snip it at four corners and turn it over and stitch it. This is a pretty thick prepuce and we will have a little more hemorrhage than usual.

Now, you see, I hold the prepuce forward in that manner, and the glans away from it; then I take a knife and shave it off at the top. There is the mucous membrane; the skin is off; the mucous membrane is not touched yet.

Now we divide this and turn it up on end; I shall then trim it down on one side, and take the other end off by paring it upward.

Then I make nicks in it in four places around, as I shall show you when I get through, and loosen it, thus making a kind of flap or curtain; we just put a stitch in each one of these and the operation is finished.

There are many different kinds of operations proposed for the relief of phymosis, but this will make the nicest cure, because we have the mucous membrane turned over. It is very important in these operations that you remove enough of the mucous membrane, because, if you do not, you will have contraction; unless you slit the membrane, as you have seen, in four or five places and then turn it over well, you will very likely have retraction.

Another method of operating for phymosis is by forcible rupture of the mucous membrane. You all know that it is that tissue that makes the trouble; it is not the integument. The skin is generally flaccid. It is the mucous membrane that has a tendency to contract. Dr. Hutchinson, I think, proposed forcible rupture of the lining membrane. A pair of forceps with long blades is passed between the prepuce and the glans and then opened forcibly and withdrawn with the blades extended. You will see, as the blades open, a rupture takes place of the mucous membrane and the disease is for the time relieved. But we find in this operation, especially in children, there is great likelihood to contraction; therefore, it is better to perform the operation as you have now seen. There is an instrument called the circumcision forceps, which is made for putting in these threads, such as are being introduced by Dr. Thompson, which also brings the membrane and skin together before you make the incision. I formerly employed them, but I have come to the conclusion that the better way is to cut off the skin entirely, then trim the mucous membrane, slit it up and turn it over. By such a process there is no such tendency to contraction.

The very contrary of phymosis is paraphymosis, which is a condition, in which the glans penis is constricted by the prepuce. In other words, the prepuce is pulled backward and contracts around the glans. I don't know a more disagreeable position for a young man to get into, or an old man either, than to have his prepuce drawn tightly around the corona, and not be able to return it. The part begins to look very angry and gets rather blue, and the man begins to be of the same color and to fear for the organ itself. It is astonishing how much love the human race do have for that part of their body; they had rather lose any thing else than part with that. There are several modes of reducing paraphymosis. In the majority of instances no operation is required. If you oil your thumbs and the prepuce and the under surface of the glans, and take the penis between your two fingers in that manner (illustrating), and place your thumbs on the glans penis, you will be able to bring the parts *in situ*.

Now, this patient certainly has a very much better looking member than he had before, and he will be able to see more of it than he has ever done in all his life.

Sometimes, in operating for phymosis, we remove the stitches a little too soon, from some irritation in the system or from some other cause, an inflammatory action is set up in the lips of the wound, between the mucous membrane and the skin, and unhealthy granulations and fungoid growths appear, which give a great deal of trouble. Therefore, it is well not to remove these stitches for at least a week.

Synovitis.

JOSEPHINE LYON, *Aged Five Years.*

History of Case.—Here is a lame leg; a sore appeared upon the ankle, and the mother put something upon it to *draw* it; then pus oozed from it; it has been discharging pus and serum; the probe goes into the joint; her physician had given her silicea, but there has been no change in her condition; the patient walks on the affected foot; the attending physician had not seen her father before her appearance in the lecture room, a little boy having come with her every time.

Prof. Helmuth said: This is a case of synovitis—inflammation of the synovial membrane, which lines the cavity of the joint, and this membrane is liable to inflammatory action. We generally find that synovitis comes from an accident, or a bruise, or an injury of some kind. This child, her father says, turned her foot, which is a very common cause of synovitis in children. There is no disease that seems to be more curable by proper internal administration of medicine than this one. The trouble is, that the child walks too much. Every time she places her foot down the weight of her body falls on the diseased membrane, and when she moves it friction results. Therefore, I say that perfect rest, combined with the internal administration of proper medicines, should be used immediately and continued. Dr. Thompson has had her in charge two or three months, and the treatment has been most judicious, but she will not get better unless she is kept still. She will continue with the medicine she has been taking, and come here again in three weeks.

Synovitis is generally curable, provided a certain amount of rest is obtained—but if, on the other hand, the inflammation is allowed to extend to the cartilages, we have a very serious disease, viz., an ulceration, which it is a very difficult matter to cure. The cartilages are supplied with blood from tufts of vessels lying upon them, and friction after bruising is liable to produce inflammation, therefore it is, that rest is necessary, if you wish to restore the part to its original integrity. The pressure and friction which belong to motion have a tendency to keep up the irritation of these articular cartilages.

Epulis.

JOHN BOWDEN, *Aged Eighty-four Years.*

History of case.—Health pretty good; swelling in the mouth, growing apparently from the gum.

After an examination, Prof. Helmuth said: Here we have a fibroid tumor or fibroid growth, properly so called; it is generally pedunculated and not sessile. A sessile growth is flat and broad. This is a fibroid tumor of the gum, which is called epulis; it bears a strong resemblance in its forms to myeloid growths, or that variety of tumor known as a myeloid tumor, and which, also, generally springs from the surface of the bone. As you see, these tumors can generally be handled with very little pain to the patient, and they can easily be removed by scraping to the bone. I shall take a pair of scissors and cut this off, and if the bone is diseased I shall scrape it. It will not take long to excise it. Or, we may put a ligature about it and let it slough off. I think it is better to cut it off and then apply nitric acid. This variety of growth sometimes attains great magnitude; sometimes they not only involve the gum itself, but they extend into the face and cause the eye to protrude, and sometimes take away a portion of the bone. It is pretty difficult, in the earlier stages of these epuli, to distinguish between them and a myeloid formation, which is more cancerous in its nature. This has been growing about a year. Epulis is very likely to grow from the socket of tooth, and it often appears on the alveolar process. It is a disease generally of middle life, although we some times find it in the aged. In this case there is a broken tooth, from which there arises a certain amount of irritation, and from that irritation the fibrous growth rapidly increases. (The tumor was cut off and the bone scraped.)

Cleft Palate.

Miss Van Houghton, *Aged Twenty Years.*

Prof. Helmuth said: Through the kindness of Dr. Houghton I have a very important case to show you, which I shall take notice of quite at length.

We have every reason, gentlemen, to feel proud of our clinics, and to feel thankful to those of the profession who interest themselves in our behalf. The four cases that will constitute this clinic are all interesting; some of them, indeed, not often encountered. Aneurism of the subclavian, phymosis, epulis, and cleft palate furnish sufficient material for a course of lectures. I must, therefore, be brief and practical in my remarks.

Perhaps there is no subject which has interested the attention of surgeons much more than this, of cleft palate. It may seem a very simple thing, whereas it is a subject of a very great deal of importance. The difficulties that surround it are numerous. We have not only the miserable condition of the patient, but we have also the uncertainty of the means of relief, as well as the fact that, after these operations, the condition of the patient is not always improved.

We will look at this lady, as I will have her go round and show you the cleft palate, and then I will call attention to the anatomy of the parts and to the different practices recommended for its cure.

The patient was here introduced.

You will recollect that the hard palate is used not only in deglutition but in enunciation. Both the hard and the soft palate not only serve as a fulcrum for deglutition, but mould the sounds that come from the larynx and give them sweetness of tone and reverberation. The first sound of G, as in "go," is always hard to articulate with a cleft palate, simply because there is no fulcrum upon which the tongue can rest, as you will see in this case, although this is an imperfect cleft. If we examine a fœtus at the sixth week the whole cavity of the mouth, the cavity of the nose, and the cavity of the pharynx is one vacuum. At the end of a few weeks more, there seems to grow from the margin of this cavity a membranous partition, which divides the nares above from the mouth below. Then from this membranous formation a vertical partitional membrane appears to come down at right angles, which divides the two nares, the one from the other. As these two sides seem to approach each other, there is a triangular space left on either side, which is afterward filled with bone from separate points of ossification, making what are termed the intermaxillary bones. First we have this rounded cavity; then from the sides of this cavity, approaching each other, and dividing it into two, we have a membranous partition formed, which seems to grow from the circumference towards the centre.

As this nearly closes, another membrane takes a vertical direction, dividing the nares. Thus the vertical membranous partition and the horizontal one come nearer and nearer together until we have the roof of the mouth almost complete, except the centre piece, which is afterward formed, and through the medium of the intermaxillary bones. These grow from separate points of ossification, and if there is an arrest of development in the hard palate, if the process of ossification does not go on as it should, and if there is any deficit in the location of the intermaxillary bones, then we have a cleft formed in the mouth, and this is termed a cleft palate. If it is a perfect cleft it is generally associated with another arrest of development, which is called hare-lip. I show you here the superior maxillary bones, and by placing them together you will see that this groove in each palate process, when the two come together, make a foramen, called the foramen incisivum, which marks the posterior boundary of the bones we are considering, which are perfectly formed about the eighth or ninth month. Not only have we the palate processes of the superior maxillary bone entering into the formation of the hard palate, but we have the palate processes of the palate bones, which form also the back part of the roof of the mouth and floor of the nares; they project backward into the mouth, and terminated in a small process, which we call the posterior nasal spine; from this, there are two muscles which hang down and form the uvula; so much for the *hard* palate. Next we have a curtain which is suspended from the hard palate, which is called the soft palate, separating the mouth in front from the pharynx behind, which is essentially muscular in structure, and which performs certain offices in the acts of deglutition and also in articulation; the muscles that enter into the formation of this soft palate are the *levator palati*—the elevator of the palate—and the *tensor palati*, or the tightener of the palate.

I have drawn on the blackboard a couple of diagrams in order to let you see as nearly as I can the relation of the parts; I have endeavored to show here a view of the bones looking from behind, as if the head were sawn off directly at the posterior nares. (Explains diagram.) Arising from the under surface of the eustachian tube and from the apex of the basilar surface of the petrous portion of the temporal, we have a mass of muscular fibres that come down and pass above the superior constrictor, thus forming that portion of the soft palate. The apex of the petrous portion of the temporal bone being a fixed point, you will see, when deglutition takes place, the action of this muscle is to draw up the palate, therefore it has its name, the levator or elevator of the palate. On the other side, I have endeavored to give you the two muscles—one the *tensor palati*, and the other the *levator palati* just mentioned. The *tensor palati* is a small muscle which lies outside the preceding and is attached to the base of the internal pterygoid plate, and winds around underneath the hamular process, and has a tendency to draw the muscle tight. (Explains the diagram.) Now, you see, these all being fixed points, whenever the act of deglutition takes place, as you swallow, the palate is drawn up. There are two other muscles which I will show you directly. Look now at the patient; when she makes an effort to swallow, you see the two sides of the cleft *come together*. I would like to ask you how it comes, that, with the *tensor palati* to lift them up, and the *circumflex palati* to pull them apart, that, when she swallows, instead of separating, the clefts come together especially when we have the palato pharyngeus and the palato glossus muscles having a tendency also to draw the parts downward and outward. These dots represent the fixed points to which these muscles act when they contact in unison.

I will tell you why—and the observation that I am about to make had eluded the most accurate observation of most distinguished surgeons of the times, until Sir William Fergusson discovered the reason. It was strange that Roux, Warren, and Velpeau, and those men who carefully examined into this subject, never seemed to arrive at the cause of this peculiarity. The reason is this: you have all seen a horse put down his head to drink at a trough, and you have seen, as he drinks, his œsophagus contracting from above until the water gets down. Now, there are three muscles, circular muscles, that enter into the construction of the pharynx, and the superior one of these is termed the superior constrictor. (Illustrating.) Let that represent the basilar process of the occipital bone, and let this represent the larynx, which is cut open from behind; and that represent the posterior nares, and this represent the palatine muscles; here we have the levator palati, the tensor palati, the palato pharyngeus which come down on the pharynx. These muscles are all associated above with this muscle which is cut open, and which is the superior constrictor of the pharynx. These muscles all being connected with the last named, when swallowing begins to take place the edges of the cleft come together from the action of the superior constrictor.

I have entered a little minutely into this description of the anatomy of cleft palate, because, after the cleft is closed, these muscles, the tensor palati, the levator palati, the palato glossus, and the palato pharyngeus then act in unison, as they ought to have done, and the tendency is to stretch the palate apart. Therefore, it is necesaary to divide the levator to avoid traction upon the sutures.

There are five varieties of cleft palate. The first, when there is a cleft on each side of the nostril, through the hard and soft palate, associated with hare-lip. This is the most severe variety. There are two clefts, one generally in each nostril; you never, or very rarely, see a cleft in the centre. If the intermaxillary bones are only partially formed, you will often find there is a protrusion in the centre of the cleft.

The second variety, is where there is a single cleft through the alveolar process, extending backward through the palate process of the superior maxillary and palate bones, and also through the soft palate.

Then we have the third variety, in which the front of the mouth is all right and the parts intact, but there is a cleft extending through from the posterior portion of the alveolar process back through the entire palate, hard and soft.

The next variety is that which we now have under consideration, when but half of the bony palate is involved, and the entire soft palate.

The last variety is that in which the soft palate alone is involved.

For the relief of these deformities a great deal can be done. Five or six years ago it was considered almost impossible to close a cleft palate in a young subject, and many times I have suggested that patients be taken away and postpone the operation until they attain their growth. But late observations have convinced many surgeons that early operations are rather preferable than those that are deferred; because, if you have to deal with an entire cleft palate, where the bony surface of the palate is involved, in early age, the bones are not ossified, and there is not so much deposit of calcareous matter; they yield readily, and, since chloroform can be given, such operations are preferable. It formerly was supposed that you could give no chloroform or ether in this operation, on account of blood dropping down into the throat, but it has been proved that anæsthetics may be administered and restoration of the palates of young children may be effected.

The operations for cleft palate are performed with knives with long handles, and the patient must be able to tolerate a foreign substance in the mouth for a considerable time, and it is well to educate them in that regard. Then the first step is to pare the edges of the cleft. You take hold of one side with long forceps and with a knife, generally bent at right angles, you shave off the margin; then you seize one of the margins and draw it out, and you pass your knife through, inward and upward, and divide the body of the levator palati muscle. You can feel the process in the back of your own mouths if you try, and if you enter the knife a little anterior to the second molar tooth, in the upper jaw, and pass it upward and inward until its point appears in the cleft by moving the handle upward and downward, you will make a very little incision in the mucous membrane and you will divide the levator palati almost completely. Then it is necessary, in a majority of instances, with a pair of blunt scissors to divide the posterior and anterior arches of the pharynx. You will see how this will relax the edges of the cleft and how they will drop down. Then stitches should be applied. In an extensive cleft of the palate, you must never try to close the hard and soft palates with one operation. In the first place, it is exceedingly tedious; second, the patient is wearied; and in the third place, the parts have not become accustomed to the traction, and thereby may readily tear out. When you close the hard palate and you find that you cannot bring the edges of the parts in apposition, then you must take a long knife with a rectangular blade and loosen up the tissue from under the surface of the hard palate for a considerable distance, and if necessary, employ lateral incisions on each side, in order to make the flaps approximate, but in no case should you make severe traction on the sutures or in the flap unless it almost comes together. I think this operation was advised by Warren, of Boston, but lately, within the last few months, Sir William Fergusson, having found great difficulty in closing the bony portions of these gaps, has devised another method of closing the hard palate, which he states is more successful than any other—that is, after having previously closed the soft palate, he introduces through the nostril a fine chisel, and divides the bony structure in such manner that the edges of the wound may be more readily brought together.

I hope you will recollect the anatomy of these parts, the means of operation, and the different steps thereof, and we will endeavor to perform it for you at an early date. It is an operation that cannot be seen very well by the class; it is too tedious and too prolonged. I would like you to recollect this anatomy, because it is important in your practice. She was removed and operated upon in the hospital.

Hip-Joint Disease.

AUGUST SISSMAN, *Aged Twelve Years, Going on Crutches Two Years.*

Prof. Helmuth said: In the last stage of hip disease the foot is turned inward; in the second stage it is turned outward. In the first stage there is not much change. This foot business is a great bugbear to students, and it always gives me great pleasure to give them such a case.

In ninety-nine cases out of a hundred—and I do not believe I say too many—you will find that hip disease has been occasioned by injury; this is the experience of medical men. But the injury is often so slight that the parents of the child, or those who have charge of him, do not notice it. A fall on the hip of a healthy child will be very apt, if it is not looked after, to produce this affection. Hip disease was formerly considered a scrofulous disorder; it used to be considered a strumous affection of the joint, but statistics prove beyond a doubt that it is persons who are not scrofulous—the most wild harum-scarum boys and girls, who are the most likely to be afflicted with the disease; and, when you trace the case, you will find that there has been at some time a bruise, or an accident has occurred.

[In this case the father said the child fell from a ladder, a distance of one story, when he was seven years of age, but did not mind the fall. When he came to grow in years his hip began to swell; it enlarged a few months after the fall; he experienced a good deal of pain during the night, and the leg and hip then showed marks of extensive suppuration with several openings.]

In all cases of developed hip disease, one of the characteristic peculiarities is that the gluteal fold of the affected side is lower than the other. In this case, there is not anchylosis, which makes a great deal of difference. You know if inflammation extends within the joint, after a time suppuration results, and abscesses open in different parts of the thigh, sometimes above and sometimes below. Then Nature attempts the cure by anchylosis, by which I mean a stiffening of the joint. It may be spurious, formed by the ligaments and tendons, or it may be osseous. If the muscles *around* the vicinity of the joint can be made prominent by an attempt at motion, even if there is apparently no motion of the joint itself, then you may be sure you have false anchylosis. If, on the other hand, the muscles cannot be drawn into any degree of tension, and the tensors do not seem to rise up, then you have true anchylosis. One method of detecting the true from the spurious is the absence of pain after manipulating in the synostosis, and the contrary in spurious.

There is a good deal of chance for this boy, but there is no hope of his ultimately recovering with a good leg. He will be a cripple, but I think, perhaps, he will get well of this condition and be able to move with moderate facility. But there must be care that he does not move too much. Let him be brought here this day three weeks. Give him silicea of the 30th, a powder every night.

It is a question upon which I have not made up my mind, how much extension of the parts will do for him. Generally, traction relieves the pain. You see, as I pull the leg down, he does not suffer. It shows that the pressure is taken off from the head of the bone, and that the caput femoris, although it may be diseased, is painful when pushed into the acetabulum. As I thrust the leg up, you see it causes him pain. Give this boy good, wholesome food, and give him the powders regularly.

In the mean time, before the three weeks have passed, I will take pleasure in lecturing to you on this subject. There is nothing like impressing upon your mind, through all your senses, the different cases that are lectured upon. Therefore, I shall be able to go on with these cases with much more facility to myself and better understanding upon your part. In the mean time, I will see that appropriate mechanical treatment is provided.

Surgical Clinic of November 14th, 1874.

Dog Bite.

JOHN SPELLMAN, *Aged Twelve Years.*

PROF. HELMUTH:

Here is a simple abrasion caused by the teeth of a dog. If it were now the heat of summer, and the hydrophobia mania was as rampant as it was during that season, we might, perhaps, consider and treat this as a case of incipient hydrophobia. A slight scratch like this sometimes results very seriously. Even when the dog has no symptoms of rabies, if the constitution is impaired, the bite may, and sometimes does, give rise to very serious consequences. There seems to be a poison in certain varieties of saliva, which, when inoculated into the system, gives rise to very great disturbance. In fact, I have never yet known the bite of a man, when inflicted upon the finger down to the bone, that did not result so seriously as to require amputation of the finger. It is astonishing how poisonous all these bites become, even in healthy persons. Among the lower classes, there are those who are so frequently engaged in fighting, that they become brutal, and snap like the lower animals; and their bite seems to be very poisonous. I have amputated more than one finger for such a wound. I have seen very disastrous consequences result from such bites or simple scratches, because the constitution is out of order, or there appears to be some process going on in the blood tending to spread the virus through the system and produce bad results.

We have cauterized this wound, so that if there is any poison in the bite it may be neutralized. The boy will be brought here again, and his constitutional symptoms will be carefully noted, and treatment applied accordingly. I think, however, that nothing further in this case will be required, but because it now appears so simple, there is no reason why it should not be carefully scrutinized.

Paronychia—Whitlow.

Mrs. Hall.—*Felon on the Finger.*

History of Case.—[This disease appeared without any apparent cause. Does her own work, and has her hands much in hot soap-suds. At first it had the appearance of a "run around," and the skin broke, and there was severe itching and burning, and the swelling seems now to be extending into the arm.]

Prof. Helmuth.—A felon, as we properly understand it, is an acute inflammation which affects the deeper tissues of the fingers and toes. Felons have been classified according to the depth of the structures which they attack. This woman states that she had an inflammation around the matrix of the nail, which is classified as the first variety of the affection.

The disease commences under the cuticle near the root or side of the nail, the pus not being deep-seated is soon evacuated; sometimes, however, the abscess takes place under the nail, in which case the pain is severe, and not unfrequently shoots up as far as the external condyle of the humerus.

The nail is sometimes punctured with a needle and the pus allowed to escape. In this case the pain is not very intense. In other varieties of felon, where the deeper tissues become affected—as the periosteum—it becomes very painful. In fact, I know of no more severe suffering than is found in the deep variety of felon. When they are in the palm of the hand the excruciating pain which the patient suffers is sometimes almost unbearable. In the earlier stages of felon it can sometimes be made to abort, that is, the inflammatory action may be subdued before suppuration is established. This may be accomplished by several means—one of these is the application of nitric acid; I have cured many in that way. Another by immersing the part in lye; another by keeping the finger in hot water; and still another to wrap around the finger the skin of a hard-boiled egg, which is between the white of the egg and the inside of the shell.

At first the patient will experience aggravation of the symptoms, but, if the application be allowed to remain, or perhaps applied at intervals, the affection will often be arrested.

These means may be used provided it has not reached the third stage, or suppuration has not commenced. If suppuration has begun, then all of these applications are worse than useless. Again, if the inflammatory action has commenced under the periosteum, the pain is more intense. In such a case the incision must be made early; but if it is above the periosteum, and especially if it is in the palm of the hand, it is better to wait until the pus forms. In other cases the formation of pus is so slow, and the pain is so severe, that it is better to open down to the periosteum, and relieve the tension by allowing the exit of blood. This person has had, first, a simple "fester" on the end of her finger, and the inflammation from improper treatment extended up the arm, as you see in the red lines extending up the forearm. This is not exactly metastasis.

We can have an extension of the inflammatory process by contiguity or by continuity. We know that there are certain organs in the body which, although at a remote distance, sympathize with each other. In such we have extension of disease by remote sympathy. We have also extension of inflammation by a continuous layer of tissue.

There has been an inflammatory action in this finger, which has been, by the application of hot water, driven to the arm; the inflammation has taken a backward action by continuity of the tissues, and now you see it located in the long flexor of the thumb. I would advise the patient to localize the inflammatory action by means of a poultice. If the inflammation is confined to the finger it is all right, but if it extends up the arm it is all wrong. Give her arsenicum internally, the 30th, every four hours. Change the poultice once every three hours. Apply the poultice as hot as it can be borne and make it of ground flaxseed. Let the arm be supported, and I think that a cure will soon be effected.

Necrosis of the Tibia.

Operation by Esmarch's Method.

EMMA SLACK, *Aged Ten Years.*

I have here an interesting case to show you; and, before she is placed under the influence of the anæsthetic, I desire to say a few words to you about her. We have got through the inflammatory process in our course of lectures, and also through some of the diseases which partake of the nature of inflammation. You will recollect that I told you that inflammatory action could extend in the bony system. We have periostitis, then osteitis, osteomyelitis, caries and necrosis. Periostitis is not a disease of the bony structure itself, but of that strong fibrous covering which overlies the bone, and not only protects it but assists in its new formation. Then we have also an affection of the lining membrane of the medullary canal. A step further we have caries of the bone, or ulceration; and, finally, the complete death of the bone. The process bears the same relation to the bony structure that it does to the soft parts. In the soft parts we have dry and moist gangrene; so in the bone we have the hard and the soft processes.

History of Emma Slack's case, now before us. Her trouble began with a pain in her knee eight months ago. She had not injured it, so far as is known. She was treated for rheumatic fever, and was sick about four weeks. When she grew better there were some purple elevations on her leg. They swelled, and finally broke and discharged. Before they opened she had a great deal of pain. The pain was worse at night and better towards morning. During the first part of the night, and until three or four o'clock in the morning the suffering was very great. These ill-conditioned abscesses would break, then others would form, and, finally, two pieces of bone came out; the largest was about two inches long and as broad as the finger. One side of the bone was smooth and the other was rough. She pulled the bones out herself.

Prof. Helmuth.—Osteitis, or inflammation of the bone itself, generally commences in the bone corpuscles, or in the calcified tissue which is around them. I have not time now to go into a description of the cell formation of bone, and as you have already had that from two or three other members of the faculty, I hope you understand all about it.

An acute attack of osteitis is a rare disease, but chronic osteitis, passing through all the different forms of caries or ulceration, is a very common affection. Of all the structures of the body the bones, as you are aware, are supplied with the smallest amount of blood vessels; but the periosteum on the outside, and the medullary matter on the inside, and the membranes that line the medullary canal, are profusely supplied with blood. Therefore, although it is rare to have a primary inflammation going on in the substance of the bone itself, yet inflammation of the periosteum or medulla is not an uncommon affection. You will find that the medullary membrane is the first to be inflamed, and afterward the disease extends to the bone. Just exactly as I have told you, the process goes on in the soft parts, so we have it in the bone. We have a molecular death, and a degeneration of the bony tissue; the molecules are carried off with the discharge, constituting caries. As I have told you before, the appearance of a carious bone very much resembles a lump of hard sugar which has been dipped for a moment in water; it is granulated, and these small granules seem to pass off with the discharge itself. Then we have the true death of the part or necrosis. Necrosis is the entire death of bone up to a certain part. The sequestrum is that portion of the dead bone which has to be separated from the living. A sequestrum is not always a loose portion of the bone. On the contrary, a portion of the sequestrum may die and yet be attached to the living bone, which is supplied with blood vessels up to the point where the sequestrum is attached to the bony surface. Then again, a sequestrum may die; nature, in endeavoring to repair the parts, may form around the dead portion a shell of bone, which becomes harder and harder, and which is called the *involucrum*, which encases the sequestrum. Through this the dead portions can be discovered by the probe, or through the cloacæ. Sequestra are also sometimes cast off, the hue of which resembles that of ossific matter which has been for some time buried in the earth. When a sequestrum is discharged the disease may be considered at its height, for nature is throwing off the dead structure, which can no longer be of any service to the economy. Often at this period, by introducing a probe, several pieces of detached bone may be readily felt.

This child has had some rheumatic affection or periostitis. Whether it resulted from an injury, or whether the child was scrofulous, I am unable to say. Certain it is that she had periostitis, then caries, and then an entire death of some portion of the bone took place. She perhaps had acute caries. You know that in chronic necrosis a patient may get about for years with one or two openings in the leg, and pieces of bone discharging; but in acute necrosis the whole bone seems to be invaded, the inflammatory process spreads with rapidity, the entire structure, up as far as the joint (and very frequently the joint itself), is involved, and there is a contraction of the tendons, and a partial necrosis of the bones in the vicinity.

What shall we do in this case? When I first saw her this morning I was disposed to recommend an immediate amputation of the leg above the knee, because I know that these prolonged operations on the bone are sometimes extremely serious; often they do not effect a cure, and, sometimes, after the best directed efforts, amputation has finally to be resorted to. Upon conversing with the mother she expressed a most decided objection to the removal of this leg. To one who does not look upon these things as we do, and to a mother in particular, who regards the child with all the affection which we naturally expect, there is something so repellant in the idea of amputation that opposition is natural. To say to a mother that such and such a part of her child must be removed—no matter how great has been the extent of the inflammation which has been going on—is a communication so awful to her, that it staggers her. When I suggested to this mother that an amputation might be necessary, she at once rebelled against it. Remembering what can be done by the method of Esmarch, and how much better we can operate by his mode than we formerly could, when the blood would pour out over all the parts, I have concluded to perform Esmarch's operation for the removal of necrosed bone, and remove as much of the disease as I can—all of it, if possible. If I find that I cannot remove all of it, and that amputation is necessary, I will remove as much as I can, close up the wound, and wait until the father of the girl can be consulted. I do not want to take upon myself the responsibility, nor give the college the reputation, nor homœopathy the discredit of operating helter skelter, without the consent of the parties interested in the case. And, besides, it would not be a proper or a right thing to do. I would not thank anybody, in my absence, to take off the leg of my child without previously consulting me, no matter how bad it was. Therefore, I give the same right to the father of this girl which I reserve to myself. He lives in Mystic, Conn. I hope it may not be necessary to remove the leg; but I am sure that extensive disease of the bone will be found, and I am also sure that the operation will be a prolonged and difficult one, because when you commence you must do it thoroughly. I propose, after the bandage is applied, to make a long incision over the tibia, and see the extent of the disease, and how much can be removed. If it is caries, the bone may be scraped. If there is necrosis (and I think there is), I will remove as much of the dead bone as I can find.

In the removal of diseased bone a great many instruments are required, particularly if the involucrum seems to close around the sequestrum; because then it is not only necessary to use the trephine, but the hammer, chisel, saws and forceps as well. Here, for instance, are a pair of lion forceps of Fergusson. The fault with ordinary bone pliers is, that they do not have leverage enough when you want to divide a hard portion of bone. Here are chisels and retractors to hold back the skin, and "holding" forceps, to secure a piece of bone, while the saw is being used.

I hope to be able to remove a portion of this bone with a single incision. We will apply Esmarch's bandage over another bandage, to prevent it being soiled by the discharge. Then we will make a longitudinal incision, and see the extent of the disease, and afterwards pack the wound with tenax, or prepared tow. This prepared oakum or tenax is now specially prepared for surgical dressing. Oakum, proper, is made from old tarred ropes. This substance is made from hemp, and the tar is afterwards put in especially for surgical dressing. It is much finer than oakum, and you get rid of the sticks and of the chunks of tar. Besides being a good disinfectant it is a good dressing for the leg. There is another article, made of fine hemp, which keeps much more moist, and has a softer feel. It is also much more impregnated with creosote, and is, therefore, a better disinfectant.

In the absence of this prepared tow you may pack the wound with lint, or you may employ cotton. But cotton is not so good as lint, because it is too shreddy, and sometimes sticks, and is difficult to get out. I heard recently quite an argument as to the propriety of using cotton as a surgical dressing. Cotton has been very highly recommended by several eminent surgeons; but there are other material that are a great deal better. If, however, you could not obtain other material, it would be proper to use cotton. In certain forms of suppurating diseases cotton seems to have a certain power over abrasions of the surface. By applying it to a burn you relieve the pain very much indeed, not only because of the exclusion of the air from the raw surface, but because there seems to be some property in the cotton applicable to the injury.

[The patient was brought in, etherized, on a stretcher.]

We put on this cotton bandage to prevent soiling the elastic one. Speaking in a general way, there are no operations more unsatisfactory than those on the bones; but Esmarch has done a good deal towards simplifying them. One of the disadvantages claimed for Esmarch's operation is this, that in wounds where there is a great deal of suppuration, and where there has been a profuse discharge of pus, there is danger of forcing the pus into the circulation. Another of the dangers which is charged against it is the oozing from the flaps, which is said to follow. The blood is withheld from the capillaries so long, that when the bandage is removed they do not contract, and injury to the flaps results. Now that the bandage has been applied you see that the leg resembles that of a dead person.

I make the first incision—putting the knife in at the tubercle of the tibia and bringing it down to an inch above the ankle. You see that no blood flows. There would be very inconvenient bleeding were it not for this bandage, because the tissues are all congested, and the cavities are full of blood. As it is, there is no special hurry; I cut through the tissues and down to the bone. I remove some of this slough with a sponge, and I see quite a large sequestrum. Now I will take a pair of forceps and see what I can do with it. (Removes bone, scrapes it.) *This* is the piece of bone that has caused the most of the trouble. The sequestrum is surrounded by an involucrum. Now I shall scrape the bone. The discharge is very fœtid and offensive.

There (demonstrating) is the new bone which has been forming around the old. I can feel it very distinctly. I will take a probe and put it down through the cloacæ. In this other opening I find that the bone has entirely degenerated and softened, and I shall therefore scrape off as much of it as possible. The little blood that you see oozing comes from the medullary cavity. As soon as the bandage is loosened you will see the blood rush into the leg like a sponge, and then we shall have a smart hemorrhage for awhile.

If this were my patient, and I had the consent of the father and mother, I should remove this leg at once. I find that the probe goes directly into the cavity of the knee joint; but having given my word not to perform amputation to-day, I will do the next best thing I can. Here is another piece of loose bone, which I will cut out by using the chisel. There is not much chance that this operation will be successful; but I will nevertheless try to save the girl's leg. This disease began in the membrane which lines the medullary canal and extended outward. The bone is not so much necrosed as you would expect to find, but it is softened, degenerated and ulcerated. You know that an ulceration is a degenerated condition of the bone—a softening and breaking down of the structure.

I will now pack the wound with tenax, bring the lips together as best I can, and await the result.

I am very glad to show you the operation of Esmarch. It has been a perfect success so far as the operation goes. I think it is especially fitted for the removal of the necrosed bone. In such an operation as this, even with a tourniquet applied, we would have had hemorrhage which would have discommoded us greatly.

The next point is to wash the wound thoroughly by introducing the nozzle of a syringe into the opening.

This patient has been under treatment about five months, and I suppose has taken all the ordinary homœopathic remedies. I shall put her on silicea immediately. That is my great remedy, and it has done more for me in cases of this kind than any other medicine I have ever used.

In packing any cavity it is well to recollect one thing—that it is better to have the substance you wish to pack with in one continuous piece, or else know just how many pieces are used; because sometimes it is very difficult to remove them, and if you leave one, disastrous results will follow. I was once called to operate for a case of necrosis at the lower end of the femur, and I found a piece of sponge that had been there for five years. It was about as big as the end of my finger. The wound had healed, but this sponge, acting as a foreign substance, had caused further irritation, which gave rise to disease after the necrosed portion of the bone had been removed.

I want you to observe the condition of the parts after the blood is let into them. As the circulation is established again, and the veins fill up, it begins to bleed. We expect that there will be a considerable quantity of oozing from this wound.

The question of amputation is one of the most serious that a surgeon has to entertain. Whether you shall or shall not remove a portion of the body is a question demanding a great deal of serious consideration and a great deal of actual experience. When this question relates to the saving of a limb, we are to inquire whether the leg, if saved, will be a serviceable one or not. It is better to get rid of a leg sometimes than save it, if the leg is to be of no service, in the way, and a deformity. If, however, you think that you can preserve a limb and make a useful member of it—enabling the patient to use it in a measure—then, of course, it is better so to do. But I am of opinion that, in a great many instances, conservative surgery saves legs, arms, and fingers that are deformities, and are only in the way. In the present advanced state of mechanical surgery it is better to remove the member than leave a deformity. You can have a patent arm so perfectly constructed that a man can drive horses or eat with it. I have seen patent legs so well adapted to their place that, if it were not for the manner in which the boot fitted, you could scarcely detect they were artificial. It is better to have an artificial leg, with which you can move about with comfort to yourself and everybody else, than have an unsightly limb which is always in the way.

Cicatrix.

SUSAN CHRINE, *Aged Seven Years.*

(*Continued from page* 25.)

This girl was here four weeks ago. The sore has suppurated and discharged since then. This was one of the tendencies to subcutaneous ulceration for which we ordered silicea. She is now a great deal better in every way. Let her return in three weeks and I think she will be cured.

Surgical Clinic of November 21st, 1874.

House-maid's Knee.

MARY MCMULLEN, *Aged Sixty Years.*

(The patient says she has a soreness and swelling below the knee; don't know that she has strained the leg.)

Prof. Helmuth.—Bursæ sometimes enlarge and inflame and occasion great suffering. We frequently see them about the wrist joint and on the dorsal tendons of the hand. When an adventitious bursa is formed along the course of a tendon the term *ganglion* is generally employed—and I do not know of any more difficult disorder to treat than the diffuse variety of bursæ. So long as we have the synovial fluid contained in the sac, and there is but slight inflammation, there is merely an unpleasant feeling when the tendons or muscles play over the cyst; but in other instances the contents of the sac increase in quantity and the fluid burrows down into the sheaths of tendons, and causes a great deal of inflammation and suppuration, sometimes resulting in gangrene and death. A bad case of ganglion is a most difficult thing to manage; but the ordinary bursæ are not so troublesome. There are a great many ways of managing them. Recollect the distinction: First, you have the simple bursa, in its natural position; then you have an enlargement of the bursa, which rises on one side of a tendon or the other; and third, we have the diffuse bursa, in which the fluid extends along the tendons, and gives rise not only to excruciating agony, but sometimes to the death of the part. A bursa in this place is frequent with women who do housework. Resting on the knees for a considerable time appears to irritate the parts, and the cyst begins to inflame. A very simple treatment is to pass a seton through the sac and let it remain until a certain amount of irritation has set in. Dr. Thompson suggests stica pulmo. I have never used it, but will try it in the next case we have. (The seton was then passed.)

Stricture of the Œsophagus.

HENRY NICHOL, *Aged Sixty-two Years.*

Prof. Helmuth.—This patient states that, up to this morning, he had not been able to get a drop of water down his throat for forty-eight hours. He has been afflicted since the first week in July last. He is a journeyman tailor by occupation. Up to the present he has always enjoyed good health. He used to carry his lunch to the shop, and about the first of July experienced difficulty in swallowing it. He could swallow liquids better than solids. He has fed on soups and broths, and has eaten no solid food since July. The food does not immediately regurgitate, but after he has eaten a little, the throat seems to contract, and whatever he happens to have in his mouth at the time he cannot swallow, and he has to eject it. For the last forty-eight hours the throat has been closed.

Those of you who have entered into the anatomy of the œsophagus know that outside the mucous coat of the tube we have a certain variety of muscle. When I was speaking to you at a former clinic, with reference to the action of the muscles which enter into the formation of the pharynx, I told you that the tendency of these muscular fibres was to contract towards the centre, and that this motion occasions that peculiarity of cleft palate which enables a person so afflicted, in swallowing, to bring the edges of the cleft together, when we would expect that the gap would be widened. The same condition of the muscular fibres extends down the œsophagus.

We have here a case of stricture of the œsophagus. You can divide this into two varieties. First, the spasmodic stricture; and, secondly, the permanent organic stricture—the latter embracing the chronic induration and the malignant variety.

In spasmodic stricture the circular muscular fibres are the seat of the affection; the disease occurs at intervals, the patient suddenly finding himself incapable of swallowing, at the same time experiencing a sensation of choking; added to this, there is not much emaciation, although there is generally great nervous irritability of the whole system. The disease is more prevalent among females than males, and is amenable to internal medicines.

One of the most interesting cases of this kind has been published in the *North American Journal of Homœopathy*, from the pen of B. F. Joslin, Jr., of New York. The patient suffered extremely, and, notwithstanding the best directed efforts, finally succumbed to the disorder. The *post mortem* examination revealed a small, hard, osseous tumor, an inch long and half an inch in breadth, with various spiculæ of bone projecting from it, situated just above the bifurcation of the trachea; a nerve was found very intimately connected with the anterior face of this tumor. Dr. Joslin considers this filament to have been a cardiac branch of the pneumogastric nerve, the irritation of which, by the presence of the tumor, caused the difficulty in swallowing. The writer says the bony tumor "did not press on the œsophagus, and was only loosely attached to the trachea; it was firmly adherent to the posterior portion of the vena cava superior; it could only be implicated in the production of the symptoms by its relations with the pneumogastric nerve."

In the one form—of organic structure—we have a vari·ty of thickening almost similar to that which we have in organic stricture of the urethra; there is a deposit of plastic material which is thrown out around the interior of the œsophagus.

Among the symptoms of this variety of stricture we see, first, the tendency to regurgitation of food; occasionally the spasm seems to close up the opening for a considerable time; and the effort to swallow any cold drinks creates a tendency to shut the œsophagus. In organic structure there is complete obstruction and always accompanying indigestion; you will also notice a peculiar expression of the face, the features being pointed and exhibiting the tokens of anguish and distress. You see, also, that the patient is considerably emaciated, and that not only the nerves that supply the œsophagus but also the inferior laryngeal nerve is affected. (A sound was then passed down to the stricture.)

What is best to be done in such a case as this? Some have been radically cured of spasmodic stricture of the œsophagus by properly administered homœopathic medicine.

The patent states that the throat contracts very suddenly on attempting to eat. Sometimes half a wine-glass of food will be swallowed and stay for some time, and then it is thrown off. It arrives at the constricted portion of the œsophagus and there it remains until further constriction throws it up.

The first direction I give this patient is never to take anything cold—not even cold drinks. He should take liquid nourishment, and take it warm. And I would recommend that, before he begins to take food of any kind, he should envelop his throat in a hot bandage. Tie around his throat, before he attempts to eat, a piece of towel, or muslin, or canton flannel, which has been dipped in very hot water, and over that apply a dry bandage. These spasmodic strictures will sometimes relax under the influence of heat. I will give him the 30th of cocculus—a dose every three hours.

In these cases of stricture of the œsophagus the patient sometimes dies from lack of nutrition.

Congenital Hernia.

ABRAHAM JONES, *About Fifty Years.*

History of Case.—(Has had hernia ever since he was a boy. Don't know what caused it. Has tried a number of trusses, but derived no benefit from any of them. Has employed several doctors, but none of them did him any good. Has no pain from it.)

Prof. Helmuth.—There are several varieties of hernia—the reducible; the irreducible, in which coats of the sac are adherent to the surrounding tissues by fibrous deposits; then, again, we have incarcerated hernia, and we have strangulated hernia. We have also a division into the congenital and the acquired variety. Again, we have different varieties of hernia, according to the locality and the nature of the parts protruded, all of which are important to be known.

This man has congenital hernia. The method of reducing hernia by the hand is called taxis. There are a great many methods of performing it. This is an oblique hernia. By that I mean a hernia which passes through both rings. The gut passes down in front of the sheath of the conjoined tendon of the transversalis and internal oblique muscle and descends into the scrotum. One portion of it feels "doughy" and the other feels as an intestine should, making it an entero-epiplocele.

In replacing the hernia you can always tell when it passes back, for it slips away from the fingers with a gurgle. There should never be any force applied in replacing a gut. A patient with a hernia can generally put it back himself, and do it even more satisfactorily than can a physician. This hernia is so old that the rings are very near together; and, although you can replace it, as you see, it slips from under the fingers. (A proper truss was ordered.)

Fistula in Ano.

ABRAHAM BAKER, *Aged Fifty Years.*

This man has what is called blind fistula—blind external fistula. By that I mean to say that he has a fistula which opens externally and is blind internally. The terms "externally blind" and "internally blind" often give rise to a great deal of discrepancy of description. It is better to say that this is a fistula which is blind internally. It opens on the outside and not within the gut.

There are cases upon record which have been cured by the internal administration of medicine, but I have never yet seen such, although I have endeavored to cure them by such means.

My advice to this patient is to get on his knees and let me cut it right out for him. (The patient decidedly objected.)

There is another way of getting rid of it—that is to introduce a ligature, tie it over a small pad, let the strings hang down, then tighten the knot from day to day.

But the best plan is first to make this a complete fistula, cut it directly through, and allow it to heal from within.

Arteritis.

LEWIS HUTTWOHL, *Aged Forty Years.*

There are certain diseases of the arteries which are obscure; but there is one in particular which is caused by an irritation of the vessel. It comes under the head of aneurismal diathesis, but it seems to be a disease which affects the elastic coat of the tubes, and is generally preceded by some affection of the heart.

Whether this belongs to that class or not it is impossible for me to say on such an examination as I am now able to make; but there seems to be a diseased action going on in the whole arterial system. When I apply my ear to his breast I hear that there is much regurgitation of blood. There is a blowing sound, showing that there is valvular insufficiency. He has a thickening of the pericardium and an affection of the arterial system. Altogether it is a case of very rare interest.

I should suppose that some of the preparations of ergotin would be advisable in this case; but as he has already been before two of the other professors, I have nothing to say as to the treatment, but will consult with them in the case.

Never be too certain in your diagnosis, when another physician has been before you, in an obscure case. If you desire to keep yourselves out of trouble in such cases, particularly when they have been prescribed for by other medical men, be sure that you call a consultation before you give a definite opinion. You do not know what damage you may do to yourselves, or to your profession, by expressing an opinion which may be directly at variance with that which has been already given by another. As doctors differ so materially in their opinions of most cases, it is always well, if you are called upon by a patient who has been visited by another physician and asked, "What do you think of my case?" to say, "I will see your medical man about it." Never express your opinion, after a consultation, *to the patient*, but always to the doctor in attendance. Never, under any circumstance, give an opinion of a case that is in the hands of a brother physician, but always let *him* perform that duty. When you are called in consultation you must take your leave of the patient *before* the consultation is held, and not return. The family physician is to receive and express your opinion, and prescribe for the patient. That is the rule, and the correct one. This running up stairs again to see the patient, and saying to him, "If I had been here day before yesterday you would have been all right," is very reprehensible, although the practice *is* prevalent among some of the profession; but they always come out at the small end of the horn. You cannot be too careful in your ethics.

Hip Joint Disease.

JOHN HART, *Aged Twenty-nine Years.*

History of Case.—(The patient says when he was about two years old he took a large dose of arsenic by accident. At the age of five had hip disease, and suffered a great deal of pain. Then two abscesses formed, discharged and healed. At the age of fourteen the abscesses broke out in his leg again. He received an injury, when thirteen, while splitting wood. The sore leg is now six inches shorter than the other; he then got the foot fast between two sticks, and on turning around felt something snap in his hip, after which there was a large swelling inside of the thigh; then two abscesses formed—one above and one below the swelling. Then several places opened and healed—one sore after another—from that time to this. Has had no splints on the leg. Has taken only constitutional remedies, such as iodine and iron. Was in Bellevue Hospital for three months, under Dr. Hamilton, who used sponge tents, which gave relief for a time, so that he was able to go back to his work—that of compositor. Worked at the case until last July. No spiculæ of bone have been discharged.)

Prof. Helmuth.—That fact makes me think that there is more caries than necrosis, or if the latter, the sequestrum is not detached.

You notice that the patient dresses the sores with paper. Paper has been largely introduced into certain hospitals as a dressing. It is not only very serviceable but it is cheap, and so easily applied that it has superseded many other dressings.

You see there are fourteen or fifteen openings on the buttock and thigh, and he has had as many as twenty-six. You see, also, that there are cicatrices all along the side of the hip.

The diseased leg is now about six inches shorter than the other.

This case is one of great interest. In the first place it shows what the human frame can suffer. When you look at that leg and see its attenuation, and remember the amount of pus that discharges from that poor fellow's thigh every day, you cannot but wonder at his power of endurance. He enjoys comparatively good health, his appetite is good, and his pulse regular. He has symptoms now coming up which resemble dropsy. This is the second or third case of hip disease we have had under treatment, and you will recollect what I told you of the different varieties of the complaint. In such a case as this we have, I suppose, not only an ulceration of the head of the thigh bone but caries, with perforation of the acetabulum.

You see here two openings on the anterior portion of the abdomen. When, in advanced hip disease, we have these openings for the exit of matter on the anterior portion of the abdomen, the indications are, that there is some more extensive disease than that of the thigh bone itself. This affection has lasted for such a length of time that there can be no doubt about the head of the bone being very seriously affected, together with the ilium.

[The doctor refuses the request of the patient to stay in the room and hear all that is said about his case.]

It is not to be wondered at that this man wants to hear everything that is to be said about his case. He wants to know whether there is the slightest hope for him. He desires to know whether he will live or die. He wants to know whether an operation can be performed for his relief. Under the circumstances I do not think that there can be. I fear that there is very little chance for his life in this world, but we may be able to somewhat benefit him. An exploratory operation in such a case as this might be advisable under certain circumstances; but not when the patient has run down so low that there is effusion taking place in the abdominal cavity, because in such the operation would not be successful, and would but add to his suffering. It seems to me, if anything can be done for him, it must be treatment which will build him up. If necessary, he may be relieved of the dropsy, and then, if the water does not reaccumulate, you may cut down to the head of the femur and perhaps exsect it. In his present condition, however, any such operation is out of the question.

Surgical Clinic of November 28th, 1874.

Varicose Ulceration.

ELIZABETH FITZGIBBONS, *Aged Thirty-eight Years.*

(A bad foot; married; has had nine children; youngest six years old.)

Prof. Helmuth.—Here is a condition of the leg occasioned by an obstruction of the venous circulation. It is occasioned by congestion, probably of some portion of the liver, which obstructs the return of blood, thus the veins become varicose. Whenever there is an inequality between the arterial and the venous supply, whether in the leg or in the heart, or in any portion of the body, then the tissues suffer. In this case ulceration will probably take place. The parts are now in a state of congestion, and are just approaching an inflammatory stage—a sub-acute inflammatory condition—which will result in ulceration, and then she will have regular varicose ulcers.

A VARICOSE ULCER

is a variety of indolent ulcer which precedes or follows a varicose enlargement of the veins of the leg or thigh; it generally makes its appearance on the inner side of the leg, and is often very difficult to cure. It resembles an indolent ulcer in a somewhat advanced stage, the edges of the skin, however, bounding the sore are not tumid; the part is blue or purple; the sore is seldom deep, usually spreads along the surface, and is oval in shape. The branches and trunk of the vena saphena are enlarged, and this varicose state prevents the ulcer from healing. A varicose limb becomes very much swollen, the coats of the veins are often thickened, the vital power is much impaired, the temperature is diminished, the parts assume that dark blue appearance to which we have already alluded, and are excessively prone to the inflammatory process, ending in ulceration, which is generally of a tedious character, although we find that the irritable sore is often accompanied with varicose veins. The pain appears to be deep seated, and extends up along the course of the vessels, and is increased by maintaining the limb in the erect posture.

Treatment.—In the treatment of indolent ulcers it is necessary that the utmost cleanliness be observed; and if the patient be one whose constitution has been impaired by unwholesome diet, exposure to a foul atmosphere, or by intemperance, these obstacles should be overcome by the substitution of nutritious, easily digested food, proper ventilation, regularity of habits; in fact, as far as possible, every effort should be made to effect the removal of the predisposing cause.

The indolent sore is capable of cure under homœopathic treatment—indeed, in some instances, without having recourse either to the bandage, straps or escharotics; and it is not absolutely necessary that the patient be put to bed, although over-exertion tends to retard recovery.

It is impossible to cure varicose ulceration without doing something for the cause of the disorder. Varicose veins may be obliterated in many ways. Unfortunately, the persons afflicted with varicose veins are usually those who have to stand on their feet a great deal. If this woman could rest for awhile, the best way to treat her would be to take two hare lip pins, pass them just underneath the vein and bring them out on the other side of the skin, about an inch apart; then twist a figure of 8 suture over each of the pins and introduce between them a tenotome flatwise on the finger, under the vein, turn up the edge and cut through the vessel. That is the best way if a patient can rest. By this method you prevent the entrance of air into the vein as well as hemorrhage. But there are some people who object to operations on varicose veins, and dislike to have pins and needles thrust into them; especially is this so in women. "Do you find this so?" "Yes, sir." You very often find a varicose condition of the veins in women before confinement, because the blood is obstructed in its return by the pressure of the fœtus, and the veins either give way or their coats dilate, and thus form varicose veins. There are also other means of obliterating varicose veins. An excellent method is the application of a paste composed of equal parts of quick lime and caustic potash, ground together, and kept in a glass stopped bottle in your office, and moistened, when you wish to apply it, with a little alcohol. This may be put on with a glass rod once a week until a sufficient inflammation is set up to obliterate the vein. It is a very convenient and effectual application. Many is the vein that I have obliterated in that manner while treating varicose ulcers, and allowed the patient to go about his business. After allowing the escharotic to remain a few moments wash the parts with vinegar, put on an elastic stocking and let the patient go. Repeat this every three or four days. Don't let the paste stay on long enough to burn through the vein. I once applied it to a patient at a clinic and forgot it while lecturing, and hemorrhage was the result. There are some medicines, which, if internally administered, will have a specific action on the coats of the vein, and the best that I know of is the Witch Hazel.

Cheiloplasty.

MISS T——, *Aged about Twenty-three.*

This young woman was before the class two years ago. I have performed four or five operations for her. She came to us first with a perfect immobility of the lower jaw. During the five or seven years that her jaws had been closed she was not able to swallow anything but soup, which she took through a straw or a glass tube. Several of her teeth ulcerated and she swallowed them; she could not spit them out. Then it was that she came to us with this cicatrix—perfect anchylosis of the inferior maxillary, an eversion of the lower lip, and a dreadful cicatrix from previous ulceration, which probably arose from the injudicious use of mercury. Fig. 1 shows somewhat the condition of the parts. The first operation, which was prolonged, tedious and bloody, was to open the jaws. Introducing a round pointed straight bistoury at the inner angle of the mouth, I divided, after a tedious dissection, all the cicatrices; then, with a modification of the instrument of Scultetus, called Westmoreland's, I gradually broke up the adhesions within the joint, and restored partially its movements. She was then placed in bed, and a gutta percha plate introduced into the mouth, between the raw surface of the cheek and the jaw, and

Fig. 1.

hickory wedges were kept between the teeth, to prevent the great tendency to contraction which is always to be expected in these cases. After three months I performed a second operation, which was as follows: First having ascertained the size of the flap, I marked its contour in the cheek. (See dotted line in fig. 2.) Then without hesitation I cut cleanly out all the cicatrical tissue. The flap was then dissected up—"jumped," as it is called—in other words, twisted on its pedicle, and sewed in place. This was very satisfactory (*vide* fig. 2). The third operation was performed about a year afterward, and consisted of cutting a lunated strip of mucous membrane and muscular fibre from the lower lip and bringing the edges of the wound together; then cutting a triangular portion from the angle of the lip, to restore as much as possible the contour of the mouth. Fig. 3 shows the result of the operation.

Fig. 2.

Fig. 3.

She now comes to us again with the cicatrix somewhat contracted and the parts grown down. I want to depress the angle of her mouth, and the first thing to be done is to dissect up these adhesions which have grown from the flap taken from the side of her face. The first thing to be done is to dissect up this from the mouth. I have used a great many substances between the jaw and the cheek in these different operations. The gutta percha did not answer; then I tried parchment; that did not do. I have brought here to-day some silver foil, which I shall endeavor to slip in after Dr. Thompson has dissected this flap up. The trouble with all these operations about the jaws is the formation of what is called inodular tissue, and the tendency of this tissue to return. I cut the whole of that out in the former operation, and the success was quite remarkable. The instrument used in this case to hold the jaws apart was Westmoreland's.

Plastic operations are those by which raw surfaces are brought together. The simplest form are operations for hare lip. In all procedures of this kind the object is to so unite the flap as to allow the circulation to proceed undisturbed. This girl has been very courageous; she has suffered many operations; and I hope that this will be the last one. I have had photographs of her taken at different stages of the cure.* I will bring them to the clinic and let you see the changes. I am very anxious to make it a success.

A surgeon must have eyes in the ends of his fingers. No other profession requires so much dexterity with the ends of the digits. A surgeon needs to educate not only the eye but the hand as well. A very good method of educating the fingers, and to improve the sense of touch, is to wind your watch every night in the dark—finding the key hole with your finger.

Hip Joint Disease.

AUGUST SISSMAN, *Aged Twelve Years.*

(*Continued from page* 60.)

You will recollect that in speaking of this case, three weeks ago, I told you that in a majority of cases of hip disease you could trace the disease back to some injury. Formerly hip joint disease was characterized as a scrofulous affection of the joint; but more recent investigations have convinced us that in very many cases it can be attributed to injury; and we often find that healthy persons are afflicted with hip disease. You recollect the appearance of this boy when he first came here, and can see that he is in every way improved. I then prescribed silicea, 30th, and said that it was better that he should have an extension apparatus made, and that such apparatus would be required before he could be perfectly cured. The extension apparatus is made and he is to have it to day. The whole aspect of the patient has improved in three weeks. You will notice that the tendency of his foot is now to invert. In its earliest stages this disease is often very difficult

* The wood cuts are accurate representations of the photographs. It will be seen that in the cuts the deformity is on the left side in Fig. 1, and shown on the right side in Figs. 2 and 3. The reason will be apparent when the fact is known that the photograph of Fig. 1 was taken *from* a photograph, while those of Figs. 2 and 3 were taken from the patient herself.

to determine. Perhaps after a run, or a jump, a strain or a fall, a child that has been active will complain in the morning of stiffness in the hip—a stiffness of so slight duration, and so slight in itself, that the parents will let it pass unnoticed; or, as the day wears on, the pain and stiffness will disappear, and the child will not feel the irritation unless it is quiet for an hour or two. The irritation may continue, and the pains increase until they become agonizing, especially at night; the leg will then become apparently lengthened, and rotated outward. The rotation outward is caused by effusion into the cavity of the joint. You can see this effect illustrated by injecting into the capsule a certain amount of quicksilver; you will find that when the joint becomes full the foot will turn outward. It is at this stage of the disease that it is so particularly trying. It is at the second stage of hip disease that the patient frequently suffers the most excruciating pains. It is because of the strain on the fibrous capsule that envelopes the head of the femur. This joint being full of fluid, the internal rotator muscles cannot act, and the external rotator muscles turn the thigh outward.

(Another patient is brought in with the same disease.)

Hip Joint Disease.

GEORGE LEE, *Aged Eight Years.*

Here you have the two stages of hip disease. As the disease progresses abscesses form around the joint and discharge in different parts of the thigh, either in the immediate vicinity of the joint, or burrow between the muscles and find exit behind. As the disease progresses further the head of the bone becomes carious, and sometimes, but very rarely, dislocates. It used to be considered, as one of the peculiarities of hip disease, that the thigh became dislocated; but this did not take place nearly so often as was supposed; more frequently the acetabulum gives way, or the head of the bone is pushed through the acetabulum.

Here you see two cases of hip disease in their advanced stages. One has been existing much longer than the other. The amount of suppuration taking place in the elder one is perfectly miraculous, and still more miraculous is the manner in which his system stands it. He has very much improved within the last week or ten days.

He feels better and stronger in every way. This boy goes to-day to the instrument maker to have the splint applied, which will allow of a certain amount of extension. There has been a great deal of improvement in both of these cases, and I hope to be able to bring them before you from time to time during the winter; if it is advisable we will make an exploratory operation upon the elder. He wants to see what can be done, and that is just what we all want. He has had a great deal of suffering. When you find abscesses in hip disease opening through the abdominal walls, it is not a favorable symptom as a general thing, because it shows that the floor of the acetabulum has been perforated, and the head of the bone must be thoroughly diseased. In such case excision of the hip cannot be performed with the same facility or success as if he bone still remained in the cavity.

Cold Abscess.

HARRIET CROSSLEY, *Aged Twelve Years.*

(Enlargement on the side of neck; has been sick over a year; the first symptoms were a swelling of the neck, which extended to the breast.)

Prof. Helmuth.—There is a gland which is called the parotid, beginning at the angle of the jaw and extending upward to the ear. This gland frequently becomes enlarged, and indurated, and then gives rise to a great deal of trouble. In other instances, where the cervical glands become enlarged they suppurate, and form cold abscesses. I mean by that, the suppuration which takes place is extremely slow, is unaccompanied by constitutional symptoms, and generally discharges some distance from the point where the inflammation commences. You will see that this is quite an interesting case. The inflammatory process began at the root of the neck, and you can see how the matter has burrowed and opened lower down. On her back she has another abscess forming, which contains fluid. I think that we can cure this girl, but it will take a good deal of time. Give her *Hepar*—the third—about two grains to be put in half a glass of water, and a spoonful taken four times every day for three or four weeks. There is no medicine that I know of that possesses such influence over the suppurating processes as Hepar, particularly when the glands are involved, and there is a tendency to suppuration in different parts of the body. By giving this medicine regularly, and following it up with silicea and sulphur, the disease may be radically cured. In cases like this I want you to bear in mind the importance of constitutional medication; I do not mean constitutional *general* treatment, as implied by ordering iron, quinine, lime and stimulants. I mean that specific constitutional medication that applies itself to the specific condition of the disease. Study out the symptoms and give the appropriate constitutional medicine, and you will cure your patient. The tendency in these diseases which we see with our eyes, and which are appreciable to our senses, is to rely too much upon local treatment. Local treatment is all very well; but I tell you, from actual personal experience, that these affections can be and are radically cured with *very little* local treatment, if you can select the right constitutional medicine—which is indicated by the symptoms of each particular case. The more you particularize, the more you scrutinize each particular case, and study the symptons of that case, and apply the medicines specifically, the more speedily you will cure your patient. To be sure this is not an easy matter. It is a great deal easier to say that you will "build the patient up," by giving him tonics; but that is not the *best way*. You must study the symptoms of each particular case. It will weary you, and discourage you very many times; there will be many drawbacks; but the man who carefully studies the symptoms of each particular case, and applies the medicine according to the proper law of cure, *he* is the man who cures his patient; and he is the man who can best instruct others in the law of cure which we profess, and believe, and know to be true. There is no denying this law of cure, because it has been tried. It has been put into the furnace and has come out pure gold. I believe that by the proper application of medicines according to our law, especially in bone diseases and this form of suppuration, can be effected in a majority of cases without the use of the knife. This may be bad for the surgeons, but we must be men enough to acknowledge the law and the facts as we find them. Don't be afraid to acknowledge a fact when you see it. It is all very well to sit down and say, "This is not so;" but the straightforward conscientious man will never be afraid to acknowledge the truth wherever he sees it, and no matter by whom pronounced. That is the principle upon which I want you all to act. Acknowledge the truth wherever you find it, no matter whether it be in this or in that college; no matter what profession, school or church, uphold it. Whenever you are convinced of a truth, and have the facts to back it up, then let the world storm as it likes; you have the truth on your side, and—"*Magna est Veritas.*"

Hypochondriasis.

MICHAEL M., *Aged Fifty Years.*

Has a "tickling noise in his head," and his "chest feels bad;" has no cough; no pain any where in particular, except sometimes in his head; sleeps well at night.

[The patient *insisted on entirely undressing* before answering any questions, saying that he wanted to have a "regular examination."]

Prof. Helmuth.—The diagnosis in this case is quite clear. He says that his appetite is good; that he sleeps well. His pulse is at 96. He is scarred all over with the marks of syphilitic eruption. He says that his chief trouble is in his chest. There is only one medicine that I know of that will help him, and that is saccharum lactis. He will have to take it pretty frequently, and diet strictly. Let him take a powder three times a day, and I think he will get over this tickling in his chest.

After the patient had retired the Doctor continued:

There is nothing much the matter with that man, but he fancies there is. You will find that patients who have suffered severely from certain forms of syphilis, and have had these sores cured by mercury, do occasionally have a peculiar form of monomania. You could see when that man came in, and began to take his shoes and stockings off, preparatory to stripping himself stark naked before you, that he had something on his mind. His pulse beats a little too rapidly, and he says that he has a pain in his head; but I think there is nothing in particular the matter. You may set it down as a rule that when a man says that he can sleep well at night, that there is very little acute suffering. People with acute pains very rarely sleep or eat well. This man is a hypochondriac. Such men may tell you that they are suffering great agony, and their statements might lead you astray if you relied upon them alone. They may perhaps induce you to give medicines to relieve a pain when perhaps there is really no symptom to be relieved. They require mental treatment. This man fancies that he is very sick. We will give him no medicine; and probably he will be back again. No class of men can exercise such an influence upon their fellows as physicians. When a physician once obtains the confidence of his patients, he can exercise over them an influence which no other man or woman can. It is often, by the exercise of this very influence on the mental condition, that you are able to perform very excellent cures. To prescribe for a patient is not the only duty of a physician; he should take a personal interest in every case; and when the patient feels that an interest in his case is developed in his physician, he will feel bound to him, and will obey him.

Many a man can go into an afflicted or distressed family, and with no medicine at all, but by his very presence alone, and through the influence that he can wield by his mental power over the sick and the suffering, or over those who are in great trouble, make his presence like a sunbeam in the house. Recollect this, and try to cultivate elevation of the mind. Sir William Hamilton left on the walls of the old University at Edinburgh these lines—"On earth there is nothing great but man; in man there is nothing great but mind." Act upon this principle, and you will be enabled to exert great influence over your patients; and combine this with the proper administration of medicines, and you have in your hands a power which it is difficult to overestimate.

Surgical Clinic of December 5th, 1874.

Prof. Helmuth commenced by quizzing the class.

Q. Which side of the body is the innominate artery? A. Generally, the right side.

Q. Please describe this artery. A. The innominate artery (brachio-cephalic) [anonyma], the largest of the vessels which proceed from the arch of the aorta, arises from the commencement of the transverse portion of the arch, before the left carotid. From this point the vessel ascends obliquely toward the right, until it arrives opposite the sterno-clavicular articulation of that side, nearly on a level with the upper margin of the clavicle, where it divides into the right subclavian, and the right carotid artery. The length of the innominate artery is very variable, but usually ranges from an inch and a half to two inches.

Q. Describe the branches of the arch of the aorta. A. They usually arise from the middle or highest part of the arch, in the following order: First, the innominate or brachio-cephalic artery, which soon subdivides into the right subclavian and the right carotid arteries; secondly, the left carotid; and thirdly, the left subclavian artery.

Q. What is an aspirator? A. An apparatus for drawing fluids from the body by the means of suction or vacuum.

Q. Describe the inter-columnar or spermatic fascia? A. This fascia is derived from the tendon of the external oblique muscle of the abdomen. On passing forward through the opening in that tendon named the external abdominal ring, the spermatic cord receives a thin membranous investment which is, as it were, continuous with the layer of so-called intercolumnar fibres, passing obliquely across the upper border of that opening; this is called the intercolumnar fascia. It is attached above to the margins of the external ring, and is prolonged downward upon the cord and testicles. It lies at first beneath the superficial fascia, but lower down beneath the dartos, and it is intimately connected with the cremaster muscle and cremasteric fascia.

Dislocation of the Femur on the Dorsum Ilii.

Henry Head, *Aged Two Years.*

Prof. Helmuth.—You remember this case, gentlemen; eight weeks ago Dr. Thompson put on a plaster bandage at the hospital. It is that of dislocation of the femur backward and upward, which occurred when the child was four months old; he was twenty months old when the plaster was applied. Four weeks ago Dr. Thompson took off the first plaster, which had been on for eight weeks, and used another. You will see that one leg is as long as the other, and he can walk, which he could not before. I cannot find that he was injured at any time, but the thigh moved in all directions—backward, and forward, and downward; it was very easily reduced by this motion of the limb. (Illustrating.) We reduced the dislocation, and this leg was then made as long as the other one. As soon as there was a slight contraction we immediately advised the plaster bandage for its relief, and it has been successful. As the child grows it will be necessary to take off this splint and put on a larger one. You see he walks now very well.

When we come to classify dislocations, gentlemen, you will find we have those occasioned by accident and those which are spontaneous. Spontaneous dislocations may arise from several causes. They are caused by muscular contraction, shallowness of the cavity in which the head of the bone rests, and again from some disease between the head of the bone and its articular surface.

The result of the treatment has been very satisfactory indeed. There is no disease about the bone; it seems to be merely a dislocation backward and upward, and if you had seen it, you would have seen—what? A shortened leg, the knee of the affected side turned over towards the opposite knee. It was not only a perfect illustration of this dislocation, but it afforded, also, an illustration of the manipulation treatment of reduction. It could be reduced directly by this simple manipulation which is now being introduced so considerably into surgical practice, viz: Flexion adduction, circumduction, and extension.

Since the introduction of anæsthetics there is no need, in the majority of cases, of applying the same force that was formerly necessary to reduce the hip, and it is found sometimes that gentle manipulation may succeed, even in a strong and powerful man, where the pulleys have not had any effect. It used to be the fashion to bleed or to administer tobacco infusion until the muscles were relaxed. This is all done away with; there is little counteracting tendency in the muscles and tendons in reducing dislocations.

This case not only is a beautiful illustration of spontaneous dislocation, but it shows how easy is the reduction. You flex the leg upon the thigh and the thigh on the abdomen; then grasp with your right hand the leg above the ankle, with the other hand take hold of the knee—you adduct it, make rotation, and then extension.

These manipulations can be employed in all dislocations, especially those of the hip. After this bone was reduced a plaster of Paris splint was applied, which in eight weeks it was necessary to remove. It is a very successful case, indeed, and a fine representation of what may be done with the immovable apparatus. Without this the patient would perhaps have become an invalid, or else would have been obliged to lie in bed with a weight at his foot. The plaster splint has effected a radical cure. You may recollect that in children the immovable apparatus is one of the very best that can be employed.

Pott's Disease, or Angular Curvature of the Spine.

ELIZABETH GERHARDT, *Aged Four Years.*

(*Continued from page* 24.)

It is ten weeks to-day since she came here. She comes from Staten Island. This disease is certainly growing better all the time. She has now been taking calcarea for a considerable time, and I will continue it at least three weeks more.

In these cases, of course, the improvement is extremely slow, and it takes years before a cure can be accomplished, but I have every reason to hope that you will see a diminution, in the projection of the spinous processes, and that the majority of the symptoms will be relieved. The object of the apparatus that you see bound to the back is to take off pressure, and that is accomplished by these crutches, which support the arms and are attached at the waist. Now, in some instances, this variety of splint is unbearable, and we have to content ourselves with medicine. Then, again, there is another form of splint, which those in better circumstances can procure; it is called "Darrach's Wheel Chair Crutch." It resembles a woman's petticoat or hoops, held upright, and padded under the arms. You take a child and place it in the centre of the apparatus, and the padded parts come directly under the arms; it takes the entire weight of the body off the spinal column. I know of three cases which have been cured by this apparatus. It was invented by Mr. Darrach for the cure of his own child.

Dr. Burdick has now a case of Pott's Disease which has been under his care for two years. He will give you the history of the case.

Pott's Disease or Angular Curvature of the Spine.

Wm. Wood, *Aged Six Years.*

Prof. S. P. Burdick.—Three years ago this little boy was first shown to me by his mother, and he was then suffering from the first indications of Pott's Disease. I advised a course of treatment, but, as this lady says, I "did not talk quite enough," always when you have any thing to say to the ladies be sure and do talking enough. The case was then submitted to Dr. Taylor, who is a very skilful physician, and he applied a splint, which the child wore for nearly a year, when the case was again presented to me without any perceptible improvement. I then advised the mother, as the brace had been properly adjusted, to continue its use, and placed the child under treatment. He has been under treatment for two years constantly; there has been no intermission, I believe. He has not failed, I think, a single day, to take the remedies which were prescribed in his case, and, during the past year, the mother tells me, she has heard no complaint from the boy whatever, although he still wears the splint, and seems perfectly well. The remedies which he has taken, from the first to the last, have been calcarea carb., 200; one dose at night, six globules, and calcarea phosphorata in the morning, ten globules. This has been his treatment from the beginning to the end. At the time he first came under my care he was having from ten to twenty passages from his bowels a-day, which Dr. Taylor informed the mother would have to wait until the spinal trouble got well, and then the disease wouldd isappear. Under the treatment of calcarea he gained a visible improvement at the end of six weeks. The trouble has decidedly improved, and his general health and strength was, from that time to the present, greatly improving, without any intermission whatever.

Now, you see, the character of this brace is very much better adapted to the case than that of the patient you last saw, but this is a very much more expensive article. He was five years old last August, and he continues to grow tall.

Stricture of the Œsophagus.

Henry Nichol, *Aged Sixty-two Years.*

(*Continued from page* 74.)

The next case is that bad case of spasmodic stricture of the œsophagus.

Prof. Helmuth.—It is two weeks to-day since he was here. (To the patient)—

Q. Can you swallow this morning? A. Yes, sir.

If you recollect, I tried to explain to you the nature of these spasmodic strictures, and I prescribed then cocculus the 30th, and ordered hot applications about his neck, and that hot drinks be taken. He says his throat feels better. He has been taking cocculus the 30th for about two weeks. There is an evident improvement in his condition, and, as I said before, cocculus has a specific influence on the muscles of the œsophagus and pharynx, and he states now, that from the relaxation of the upper part of his throat he begins to feel more comfortable. The law in medicine is, to let well enough alone, although the temptation is, when you have a case that is doing well, to change the medicine or to resort to other means. Particularly with young practitioners is this a strong temptation; they prescribe for a patient and think that the medicine must act in a short space of time, and if very deeply interested in the case, they think their reputation is at stake. I was so. When a young practitioner is called to a case, he is very anxious for its success, and he studies it up very thoroughly, and finds the medicine he thinks is proper; he gives it to the patient, and expects to see immediate relief. If the expected improvement is not immediate, he takes down the books, supposes he has given the wrong medicine, and goes back the next morning and changes it. But I began to find out, as I grew older, that it was a good thing in medicine to let well enough alone, and to give the medicine opportunity to act. One reason why doctors can never treat their own families successfully in severe cases, is, that they *know too much.* Very often physicians think they overflow with wisdom, but when they come to prescribe for their own families their egotism falters. They give a dose of medicine to their child, they take out the books and find another remedy which they think better than the first, and so they desire to change the prescription. There is another thing to be remembered; when a patient is getting better by nature, if you have common sense, let nature continue, you can have the honor all the same. Don't interfere with it. The law is, and write it down, that when a patient is improving, continue the same medicine until you are sure it has exhausted itself, and when the patient begins to get worse, do not think it is an aggravation for the Lord's sake. Many split on this rock. Nothing makes me so angry as to have a person come into my office and say, "Doctor, I have been worse ever since I took that medicine," where I know medicine had nothing to do with it.

As to this patient, he is getting better, and I believe cocculus will relieve this stricture, so I will continue it for two weeks more. We will go on and give you this medicine and you will come back in two weeks. He asks me if I am going to put something into his throat. I will not. I never, in spasmodic strictures, put instruments into cavities where there is a liability to spasm; that very often aggravates the case. I say that it is a triumph of surgery if you can by internal administration of medicine cure a disease which formerly was treated only surgically. I do not mean to put any instrument in your throat to-day; but you must come back in two weeks. If you should get worse, come next Saturday; but, if you think you are getting better, stay two weeks.

The great fault of teaching in medical colleges is this—that you are led to believe, when you are called to see a case of disease, it will be easy to diagnose and to treat. The descriptions are so simple in the books that little difficulty is apprehended by the student as to his capability to perform professional duty. This is wrong. Often in diseases there is such a similitude that it takes the closest power of discrimination and the greatest wisdom to diagnose one from another. You think it is easy to diagnose a dislocation of the lower jaw. Yet even this has been mistaken. There are difficulties in all cases, but the man who overcomes the difficulties, makes the best physician. The greater the difficulty on the one hand, the greater should be the incentive to study on the other. Don't you dare, when you have gone home after curing a simple case, to think that you are a great doctor; because *you are not*, for diseases get well of themselves. Take a bad case and bring that through all right, and then you can prove yourself competent. When you are an M. D., when you think you have passed through the green room and are regularly empowered to encounter all the diseases with which the world is affected, do not, because you cure one or two of them, think you are a great man.

The next case we will have is a small tumor over the eye. It is not much, but it is the little things in this life that make the great ones; it is the atoms which make the world; it is the motion of those particles which make light, heat and electricity, and the man that disregards the little things in life, is not the man that can overcome the great ones.

Sebaceous Tumor.

HATTIE ANDREWS, *aged* 15 *years.*

Here is a tumor that lies directly over the external canthus of the eye. Sometimes these small tumors which grow in the neighborhood of the frontal bone, or skull, from the pressure they exert, have a tendency to absorb the bone, and a tumor like this one pressing down so on the bone may absorb it. This is a favorite way to remove them. Raise the skin, like that, and then enter the knife, with the back downward, and cut from within; that makes a clean cut down through the tissue. After you have made your incision, take a pair of forceps, and raise up the skin. These things stick very tight sometimes, and are sometimes very difficult to get out. (The tumor was dissected out.)

Sebaceous tumors have different kinds of sacs. In some you have seen the envelope is very thin; in other instances the sacs are perfectly firm and hard; and still in other instances they adhere not only to the superimposed structures, but also those below. This patient now should be principally treated with cold water dressing. No, do not give her any medicine. I know she will get well without, and if I were to give her medicine and she were to recover, I might suppose that I was very scientific. Common sense in medicine, is a great thing, gentlemen. The trouble is, we are apt to lose our common sense when we come to get too much science. It is not the most studious physician who makes the best practitioner. It is an acknowledged and accepted fact that the most distinguished men in the profession for their learning, are often the least practical when they come to the bedside.

PROF. HELMUTH [To a student of the class]:

Q. Now, sir, ether you say is an anæsthetic. Who introduced it? A. Dr. WELLS, of Hartford, Conn.

Q. Are you sure it was Dr. WELLS? What about Dr. MORTON? See page 17.

Q. Who introduced chloroform? A. Prof. SIMPSON, of Edinburgh.

Q. What are the rules for giving ether. In the first instance, must the patient have a full or empty stomach when he takes ether? A. An empty stomach.

Q. Then what is the next thing. This gentleman says they must let atmospheric air in where a patient is anæsthetized? A. It is not necessary. The rule for the administration of ether is this: that if the ether be pure, there is no necessity for atmospheric air. The best precaution is to have the patient fast for at least three hours, and after fasting he should have, about half an hour before administering the ether, a stimulus in the shape of brandy, or about eight to ten grains of bromine of potassa. Then the anæsthesia must be carried to insensibility.

Spencer lays it down as a law, and as one of the principles, that he never pushes anæsthesia to more than insensibility. When a purple skin and stertorous breathing appear, then it is time that it should be suspended.

With chloroform the case is very different. In chloroform there must be always an admixture of atmospheric air; the patient to be watched carefully and very closely. Fluttering of the heart and spasmodic breathing are bad signs with chloroform, and the trouble is just here—a patient may pass from life to death before the operator is scarcely aware of it; and a patient in apparently good health may take his seat in the chair, and the chloroform may affect him in such a manner as to make death imminent, or he may expire at once. It is for this reason that I am opposed to giving chloroform, except, perhaps, in cases where it seems to act remarkably well, such as the relaxation of the muscles in obstetrical practice. I argue that it is better for the operator, that the patient take ether, than to run the risk of a sudden death. From ether you have the stage of insensibility coming slowly, it is true, but still it is a better and a safer practice to resort to than the use of chloroform. If I am operating on a patient under chloroform, I have to be thinking of the chloroform as well as the operation; but if I am practicing with ether, I am free of care, and that is a great deal.

Surgical Clinic of December 12th, 1874.

Prof. Helmuth to the Class.

Q. What is the difference between phymosis and paraphymosis? A. Phymosis is a preternatural constriction with elongation of the prepuce, in front of the orifice of the urethra. Paraphymosis is the reverse of phymosis—the prepuce becoming retracted behind the corona glandis, leaving the glans uncovered.

Q. How many stages of hip disease are there? A. Three distinct stages.

Q. How is the foot in the first stage? A. It is generally not much altered in position.

Q. How is the foot in the second stage? A. Abducted and rotated outward.

Q. How is the foot in the third stage? A. Assumes a position directly opposite to that noticed in the second stage. It is rotated inward, shortened and abducted; the toes only touch the ground.

Q. What is the difference in the diagnosis between fractures and dislocations? A. In fracture there is increased mobility, crepitus, and when the broken extremities are placed in apposition, they will not thus remain without external support; while in dislocation or luxation there is unnatural rigidity, and the displaced part remains fixed. There is likewise discoloration, pain, and swelling; at times, temporary paralysis. The limb is shortened, very seldom lengthened. When the dislocated end of the bone can be felt, it will be found in an unnatural location, and a depression be detected in the place that the extremity of the bone occupied.

Neuralgia of the Stump.

Thomas Whiting, *aged* 26 *years.*

History of Case.—Lost his arm ten years ago, by machinery. The arm was caught in a belt and taken round a shaft. Amputation at the middle third took place three days after. The stump now pains him all the time, and has for the last two years. The suffering is worse at night than in the day. The cicatrix has contracted on the end of the bone. There was no pain for a number of years after the operation; but the parts began to be sensitive when the integument began to contract over the bone. At the time of the amputation, mortification was rapidly extending up the arm.

PROF. HELMUTH:

That arm is a very good text for two or three lectures. In the first place, it is a good text to speak from, with reference to what is called traumatic gangrene. You will recollect that, when I was speaking of the terminations of the inflammatory process, I stated that in dry gangrene or in the ordinary forms of mortification, it was necessary, before amputating, to wait for the line of demarcation, and that in other cases, it was just the contrary; and when we had traumatic gangrene, which extended rapidly, and the life of the patient was at stake, amputation should be performed, and the sooner the better. If you will put your finger on the end of this stump, you will feel that the bone has been sawn off diagonally, that the bone is sharp at that extremity, that the tissues have adhered thereto, and that there has been a contraction of the flap. There is a difference of opinion as to the period and point of amputation in traumatic gangrene. Particularly in those injuries which result from machinery, where the parts are bruised, and crushed and lacerated to a pulp, and there is no way whatsoever to relieve the patient, and the gangrene seems rapidly extending itself—then to wait for the line of demarcation is to wait for death, and to give the patient over to it.

If, on the other hand, we have dry gangrene, then it is wrong to perform an amputation until the line of demarcation is fully formed. In such gangrene as this man had, amputation must be resorted to within one or two days. There may be a primary amputation performed; but after an amputation, no matter how skillfully performed, certain untoward results may follow. For a considerable period of time after an amputation a patient may consider himself cured; but some unhealthy action may take place in the stump, which gives rise to intense pain, which may be easily accounted for. There is a great tendency in all tissues during the healing process to contract, and during contraction there is a tendency to adhesion to the end of the bone. This patient says that for seven or eight years he enjoyed perfectly good health, and but little pain. Then, two or three years ago, he began to feel pain and soreness on the under surface of the arm, and then he referred his suffering to the amputated fingers. There is frequently this peculiarity attending amputations—that the patient seems to have sensibility conveyed to his brain through the stump, as it was through the limb before it was taken off; and sensations at the end of the fingers are apparently felt as well as they were before the arm was amputated. Here has been a contraction of the cicatricial tissue, and an adherence to the bone; and as the tissues adhered to the bone, they embraced within them certain filaments of the median nerve. The median nerve on the under side of the arm is included in this cicatrix, and therefore he will tell you that he has all these nervous sensations. In other words, he has neuralgia of the stump, which is worse at night, which gives him apparent sensitiveness at the end of the fingers, and which is always aggravated in bad weather. He can tell by that stump when a storm is coming. The pain is always worse at night, and is then of a shooting and darting character.

What can we do to relieve this neuralgia of the stump? If it is simply idiopathic, and caused by the division of the nerves alone—if there are no mechanical troubles connected with it, there are medicines which will be of the greatest possible service to relieve the patient. I may mention here, that during the battle of Waterloo the Marquis of Anglesy had his leg shot off; it was amputated on the spot, but for five years he suffered very severely from neuralgia of the stump, trying many remedies to relieve the pain, but all in vain; and I assure you that this pain is almost unbearable at times. Finally he sought Hahnemann in Paris, and by him was cured of the neuralgia by internal medication. That is a fact in history, and there is no denying it. In a case like this, however, where the nerves are involved in the contracting tissue, other means may have to be resorted to, to produce the desired effect. Before I speak of the mechanical causes of this neuralgia of the stump, I will relate a case of the affection which was cured by the use of a medicine but little known.

I was called across the river to see a man suffering from neuralgia of the stump. He had recovered from a thigh amputation; the stump had healed, and seemed sound, and yet the pain he suffered was perfectly appalling. He had tried a great many medicines, such as belladonna, the acetate of copper, ign., cicu., zinc, hydrochlorate of amm., morphia, and others of that class of medicines which act upon the nervous system, and which, according to the symptoms in each particular case, will often produce relief. In this case, however, all the different remedies were tried without avail, and the patient was in such despair that he often thought of committing suicide. He had tried many doctors, of all schools, and had given himself up as a hopeless case. He was a great smoker, and as he stooped one day to light his pipe from a scrap of French newspaper, he read of a case of neuralgia of the stump which had been cured by eating onions. He immediately sent out and procured three large ones, and ate them; and for the first night in two years he slept. He continued this treatment for several days, and was able to sleep every night. Then he thought he would try the tincture of *allium cepa;* and he took the tincture with almost the same effect. He got into the habit of eating an onion every night before going to bed; and finally cured himself of the neuralgia. This medicine, therefore—*allium cepa*—must be put down as one of those for neuralgia of the stump, and it is well to recollect it.

With respect to the patient before us, it would seem that we must do something to prevent further contraction of that cicatrix. We will give him some internal medicine, and apply a lotion to the stump. If that does not do, and the pain becomes aggravating, the adhesions must be loosened from the bone by an operation. That will certainly relieve him, and then internal medicines must be given. If a mechanical obstruction is the cause of the neuralgia, we must resort to mechanical means for relief. I will prescribe for two weeks: the tincture of *allium cepa*, five drops, to be taken four times a day in a tablespoonful of water; and I will have applied to his arm at night a simple onion poultice. Take a good sized onion, chop it up fine, put it into a rag, and tie it on to the stump at night.

Broken Needle.

MARIA REED, *aged* 16 *years.*

With a broken needle in her hand.

She has the blunt end of the needle in her hand; and if it were within reach, and you could determine its position, it would be high time *then* to cut down and take it out. But now I cannot even feel the needle, and do not know where it is located, and it would be improper to make an exploratory operation in the palm of the hand in search of it, when we do not know in what direction to probe. Needles have entered the palm of the hand, and have come out at the shoulder; they have entered at the knee, and I have taken them out at the chest. And so with bits of glass and splinters. Metallic substances, especially, have a tendency to wander through the system. Until this needle comes nearer the surface it would be wrong to meddle with it. She will feel it somewhere near the surface after awhile. It may move quite fast. As it does not give her any inconvenience, it is better to wait until it makes its location known. She need not worry herself about it, for it will not hurt her. This looking for needles when you don't know where to find them, is a very unsatisfactory thing, and very unsuccessful.

Hip-Joint Disease.

KATIE PAULDING, *aged* 3½ *years.*

History of Case.—Has been lame since she had a fall, six months ago. She was standing in the door, a dog ran under her and pushed her legs apart, and she fell heavily on the floor. She immediately arose, but walked lame, and has been lame ever since. For two weeks she has not been able to walk at all. She has a great deal of pain at night.

PROF. HELMUTH:

This is a rapid case of hip disease. You observe one foot is turned out, and the leg seems longer than the other. She complains a great deal of pain in the knee, and the mother supposed that the injury was in her knee, until Dr. Thompson told her that it was in the hip. This patient fell and bruised the articular cartilages, and from that time to this, inflammatory action has been taking place. The leg has a tendency to turn out, and is half to seven-eighths of an inch longer than the other. If this patient had been taken in hand the moment she fell, and put on her back, an application of arnica applied to the hip, and arnica administered internally, the disease would probably have been prevented. But the parents of the patient, not knowing the re-result of exercise in an injury to the hip, did not have any thing done, and permitted the child to exercise as usual. The pain increased and became aggravated at night, and it must now be looked after, because it is almost impossible to arrest the disease after it proceeds to the second stage. This child must be kept on its back. Every pressure, every motion of the head of the bone in its socket, has a tendency to bring together two surfaces which are already inflamed and irritated. Put the patient in bed; but for the present apply no extension, because I am not quite certain whether or not the effusion has yet taken place. Give the child perfect rest. Apply arnica on the outside and internally, and also the 3d trituration of lithia. This is recommended in the first stages of hip disease; although I have not yet had any experience in the use of it.

Hip-Joint Disease.

ALBERT SISSMANN, *aged* 12 *years.*

(*Continued from pages* 60 *and* 85.)

[Boy enters walking, and moving well.]

You will recollect that this boy has been here before for hip disease. I will to-day show you the principle upon which this splint acts. There are a great many splints which are made and applied for hip disease. This is a plain splint, and is what is called Bauer's splint. I use it very often for this class of cases, because many of the other splints require to be held in place by adhesive straps, and it takes a great deal of care to keep them adjusted. Here is a crutch, and a strap so arranged as to create counter extension. Here are two cylinders which are attached to the shoe, and are so arranged that by turning the key you can draw one from the other and thus make extension. You can see the foot move as I turn the key. He turns the key every day. You can see that his foot is now brought almost to the floor. You also see an immense improvement in his general health.

There is another splint which is a very excellent one, and that is the splint of Dr. Taylor. In that, the foot does not come to the ground at all. An iron extends below the shoe, and the patient walks on the iron. There is no jar given to the foot, for all the weight comes on the iron bar. Then there is the splint of Dr. Sayre, made on the same principle, with the exception that it has no shoe nor bar, and is held by adhesive straps. Then there is the old splint of Dr. Davis, who was the originator of these splints, and the first man who gave an impetus to the application of extension and counter-extension in hip disease.

Nævus.

IDA TELLER, *aged* 5 *months.*

(*Continued from page* 13.)

We have here the child with the nævus that was operated upon at the first clinic this winter. It has now been healed up for about three weeks. She is brought here to-day to satisfy your curiosity. It has certainly very much improved in condition since it was operated upon.

Hernia.

JOHN THOMAS PARRY, *aged* 6 *years.*

PROF. HELMUTH:

It always gives me a great deal of pleasure to show a case of rupture, for it gives great facilities for "quizzing" you about it; and as I have said before, I enjoy these examinations probably a great deal more than you do.

This child was born with this rupture. It is not a hydrocele, for hydrocele begins at the bottom of the scrotum; hernia begins at the top. Hydrocele has no cough impulse; hernia has a cough impulse. Hydrocele is translucent, when we hold a lamp behind it; hernia is not, except in certain cases. Inversion of the body sends the hernia up, but when the patient resumes his position the hernia returns. If you had hydrocele, you might hang by your feet forty days and it would make no difference with the tumor. There is in this child a predisposition to hernia. He has congenital hernia. I should advise this patient, with such rings as those, to undergo an operation for its relief. You know that there is what is called the radical cure for hernia; but it is not adapted to all the varieties. But in such a case as this, where the rings are so large, I think that it is advisable to try the radical cure operation. The ring is so extensive that, as you see, I can pass my finger into the internal ring. It would be almost impossible to keep this gut up with a truss, the rings are so distended. The method of performing the radical cure is simply this: You pass a needle, threaded with wire, through the internal pillar of the ring, bring it out, twist it; turn it back through the external ring, bring it up again and twist it. This sets up sufficient inflammation to invaginate the scrotum. That is after Wood's method. Wurtzer's method consists in taking a plug of wood made on purpose, with a needle to run through the block. You push the block into the scrotum and hold it there; then push the needle out through the abdominal wall, and screw a clamp on top of the needle in order to retain it until suppuration is established.

What can be done in this case. If allowed to remain as it is, it will strangulate, and give him a great deal of trouble. If he grows up, it will still give him a great deal of anxiety. Therefore, I advise that an operation be performed on the child. He will have then to be kept very still. It is an operation not always free from danger; but, at the same time, it affords the best means of being permanently cured. Take the child home and talk to his mother about it, and then come and see us again. If you do not conclude to have it performed, we will then do the next best thing. But it has gone so far that I think the radical cure operation is the better.

Recollect, that there is congenital hernia and acquired hernia; and that it is not necessary that congenital hernia should develop itself at birth.

Sebaceous Tumor.

HATTIE ANDREWS, *aged* 15 *years*.

(*Continued from page* 97.)

DR. THOMPSON says that he was sent for on Sunday night to see the patient; found the right eye swollen up and closed, and suspected erysipelas; the pulse was at 120; and he prescribed aconite and belladonna. On Monday night, the eye was still more swollen. Forty-eight hours after the operation the inflammation had extended to both eyes. He withdrew the sutures, and there came away at least two tablespoonsful of sanguineous pus. The wound gaped open. At the time of the operation there was a small artery which bled considerably, and was not tied, hoping that the hemorrhage would stop without a ligature. But there was some secondary hemorrhage, and the wound filled with blood and pus, so that it was necessary to open it. Afterwards slight compression was made with plaster; and now she is doing very well. She was brought here on Tuesday morning, and has been here ever since. She can now open her eye, and there is scarcely any swelling. These sebaceous tumors sometimes undergo a spontaneous cure. Sometimes an inflammatory action sets up in the sac and the contents are discharged. But then there generally remains an unsightly scar. Therefore make it a rule, in removing sebaceous tumors, to remove as much as possible of the cyst wall, or else you may have a reproduction. But the cyst is not of sufficient importance for you to remove it altogether, if portions of it lie in very close proximity to important structures, because, if you remove three-fourths of the cyst, in a majority of cases, the other one-fourth will pass off with the discharge. In the performance of the operation you must never injure any other part. That is a law, you must always follow, in whatever operation you perform.

Surgical Clinic of December 19th, 1875.

Prof. Helmuth quizzes the class on hernia abdominalis or abdominal hernia.

Q. What do we understand by hernia? A. Protrusion of the contents of any cavity of the body.

Q. What is the difference between congenital and acquired hernia? A. Congenital hernia may occur soon after birth. At this time the intestine or omentum passes out of the abdomen, accompanies the testicle in its descent, and becomes lodged in the pouch of peritoneum which forms the tunica vaginalis testis before its communication with the general peritoneal cavity has become obliterated. Acquired hernia occurs from lifting, straining, or making violent muscular exertions of any kind.

Q. What is an inguinal hernia? A. It is that in which the bowel protrudes at the groins or through the abdominal rings.

Q. What is a direct inguinal hernia? A. It is that in which the bowel protrudes through the abdominal wall and the external ring.

Q. What is oblique inguinal hernia? A. The bowel protrudes through both rings and through the inguinal canal.

Q. What is the difference in the coverings of the oblique and direct inguinal hernia? A. They are the same, except in the direct, the conjoined tendon is substituted for the cremasteric fascia.

Q. If we find that we have a tumor beginning at the bottom of the scrotum, how would you diagnose whether it were a hernia or a hydrocele?

1. *Hernia* is almost invariably opaque, the only exception being in case of a large fold of intestine distended with gas and covered by thin integument.	1. *Hydrocele* simulates hernia, but differs from it by being more or less translucent.
2. The tumor is always varying in size, and can generally be made to disappear by pressure.	2. The tumor is constant.
3. The cord can never be distinctly felt in any part.	3. A part of the cord can be felt distinct from the tumor at its apex.
4. The tumor is enlarged upon coughing or exertion.	4. Hydrocele, unless congenital, does not enlarge upon or feel the impulse of coughing or exertion of the muscles.
5. The testicle can be felt distinct and separate from the tumor at the lower part of the scrotum.	5. The testicle can scarcely be felt, if at all.
6. Hernia appears suddenly, is developed from above and descends.	6. Hydrocele forms gradually, and is developed from below upwards.

Q. How would you diagnose varicocele from hernia? A. In the varicocele the swelling is not reducible, and has the feeling as of a bunch of worms.

Q. What is the difference between enterocele and epiplocele? A. In the first the intestine alone is displaced; in the latter, the omentum alone is displaced.

Q. What is entero-epiplocele? It is that in which both the intestines and omentum protrude.

Q. What is encephalocele? A. Hernia of the brain.

Q. What is pneumocele? A. Hernia of the thorax.

Q. What is reducible hernia? A. One in which the protruding bowel may be replaced into the cavity from which it came, either spontaneously or by taxis.

Q. What is irreducible hernia? A. When there exists a protrusion of the bowel which cannot be returned to the abdomen.

Q. What is strangulated hernia? A. It is that form of hernia in which the bowel is so pressed upon at the point where it passes through the walls of the abdomen, that it is strangled or constricted, which prevents the contents of the intestines from passing to the anus, and the venous circulation is impeded.

Q. What is crural or femoral hernia? A. It is a dropping down of the bowel behind Poupart's ligament, and appearing as a tumor at the upper part of the thigh.

Q. What is the difference in diagnosis between femoral and inguinal hernia? A. In the femoral hernia the finger can be introduced into the inguinal canal. Poupart's ligament cannot be made out, even though the gut has ridden over it. An inguinal hernia lies inside of the spine of the pubis.

Prof. Helmuth said:

Psoas abscess may, in rare instances, be mistaken for femoral hernia.

But the many presenting symptoms of spinal disease, the slowness and variability of progress, the fluctuation, and the part at which the abscess points, which, in the majority of cases, is outside of that which hernia protrudes, serve to form the distinctions necessary for diagnosis.

An *enlarged gland* has been mistaken for hernia by most distinguished surgeons. Hamilton records a case in which several days elapsed before the diagnosis was made out, the delay causing the death of the patient. Sir Astley Cooper also mentions two fatal cases of the kind. The absence of cough impulse, the solidity of the tumor, history of the case, and the constitution of the patient, must be our chief guides in these cases.

Q. How would you diagnose sarcocele from hernia? A. By absence of cough, impulse, and the non-implication of the spermatic cord, and the history of the case.

Q. What do you understand by the term Aneurism? A. A pulsatory tumor, which is filled with blood, partly fluid and partly coagulated, and whose cavity communicates with the arterial canal.

Q. What do you understand by the term True Aneurism? A. It is formed by the dilated coats of an artery forming a pouch, or sac; this sac is composed of all the arterial coats.

Q. What is the difference between a true and a false aneurism? A. By true aneurism we mean a partial dilatation of all the coats of the vessel. By false aneurism we mean expansion of the one, the rupture of the other.

Q. How is the dilatation of aneurism classified? A. Into *cylindroid*, *fusiform* or *sacciform*.

Q. What is the difference in these three dilatations of aneurism? A. In *cylindroid* the expansion is abrupt and uniform. In *fusiform* the enlargement is spindle-shaped. In *sacciform* the dilatation is partial, and arises from the side of the vessel.

Q. What is hæmostatics? A. The arrest of bleeding. It may be natural or may be artificial.

Q. What do we understand by torsion? A. Twisting of arteries to arrest bleeding.

Q. What is tetanus? A. Permanent spasmodic contractions, or spasm of the voluntary muscles of a portion or nearly the whole of the body, rendering it stiff and straight.

Q. How many kinds of tetanus are there? A. Idiopathic, produced by exposure to cold; and traumatic, produced by bodily injüries, particularly the injury of a nerve.

Q. What is trismus? A. When the spasm presents itself in the muscles of the neck, throat, and jaw.

Q. What is episthotonos? A. When the muscles of the back are affected, the patient is drawn backward into the shape of a hoop, and rests on his head and heels.

Q. What is emprosthotonos? A. It is exactly an opposite condition of episthotonos, the body being bent or drawn forward.

Q. What is pleurosthotonos? A. It is when the muscles of the side of the body are affected with tetanic spasm.

Hypospadia and Retained Testicle.

Q. What is hypospadias? A. When the urethral opening terminates or exists in the course of the canal on the lower side of the penis.

Q. If the urethra terminated on the upper portion of the penis, what would it be called? A. Epispadias.

I propose to present to the class to-day a case of hypospadia, with retained testicles, which has been operated upon once or twice, without success. I might say that all operations are nearly useless in this class of cases. This young man has been a student of medicine, but has been rendered unfit for work by this deformity. Both of his testicles are retained and sore. In a majority of instances the operations in such cases are unsuccessful. I bring him before you to show you an aggravated case of hypospadias, and at the same time to state a very peculiar fact, which is this: that this man has all the sensation of passing semen, as if his parts were in a normal condition, and that the sensation is attributed or referred by him to the *end* of the penis. The semen and urine pass through an opening in the membranous portion of the urethra. The patient has been operated on by Dr. Tiffany, of Baltimore, but the operation was not successful. The opening is now in the perinæum. The patient is very destitute, and I thought that I would bring him before the class, that you might have an opportunity of seeing the case; and if any of you choose to assist him, with ever so little, he will be grateful. I shall therefore ask him to exhibit himself to you. It is rare that you can see such an aggravated case of hypospadia, and this complicated as it is with by retained testicles.

Patient is brought in.

HENRY WILSON, *aged* 37 *years.*

Q. You have had this malformation from birth? A. Yes, sir; from my birth.

Q. Before you were operated upon, how far back in the

urethra was the opening through which you passed water? A. Three and a half inches.

Q. As you came from boyhood to puberty, did you have sexual desire? A. Yes; and rather prematurely.

Q. The scrotum was well developed before the operation? A. Not very well. There was some redundancy of tissue. The testicles never came down.

Q. When you have emissions of semen, do you have pain in the testicles? A. Not at all.

Q. Do you have any unpleasant feeling in the testicles? A. Yes, preceding the emission. It makes the left testicle painful a long time before there is an emission.

Q. Then you do not have any such trouble in the right testicle? A. I have no evidence of any right testicle having an existence. I was operated upon by Dr. Tiffany, in Baltimore. His object was to make a flap out of the scrotum.

Cold Abscess.

HENRY PICKETT, *Aged Five Years.*

Has had a swelling on the lower jaw for about three weeks. His mother thinks he has a decayed tooth, but has not complained of the tooth-ache.

Very often in children we find that where there are diseased fangs of a tooth, or where the alveolar processes of the inferior or superior maxillary bone are very thin, an irritation is aroused which extends along the root of the tooth, and connects itself to the periosteum and we have the formation of cold abscesses. This boy has a cold abscess, caused by an irritation at the root of the tooth, external to the periosteum, in tissues so yielding that very little pain is experienced. It is not yet time to do any thing with this abscess. The suppuration is slow, and has all the characteristics of a chronic abscess. There is very little pain, but the suppurating process is proceeding. I can detect slight fluctuation there now, and by introducing a needle perhaps I could withdraw the matter; but that opening would not be sufficient; the pus would not be fully discharged, and a second incision would be necessary; and the desire of the mother is to avoid a scar. Therefore, I think that we will leave this as it is for several days. Bring him back at the end of a week; if it has fully suppurated, we will withdraw the pus and leave nothing but the puncture. Give the boy three powders per day of cal. carb., 30th trituration.

Dementia.

JOHANNA REGLAN, *Aged Four Years.*

History of Case.—The child can use her hands, but does not know how to feed herself; does not know how to walk; has a vacant look; is very quiet.

PROF. HELMUTH:

Here is a case which does not properly belong to my department. There is no surgical disease here. There is a deficiency in mental development, of brain structure. There is such a lack of brain and nervous power that the child, although it sees and hears, is not able to accomplish the simple act of prehension, and does not even know how to eat. She has the use of her hands, but does not understand how to take up food and put it in her mouth. In a case like this, nothing but a long course of treatment can be expected to do any good. The prognosis is extremely unfavorable in every way. The peculiarity is this: Here is a healthy woman, with a healthy husband, who has had several children that are perfectly well; yet, without any known cause, she is delivered of a child mentally deficient. It is not my province to enter into this subject—which is very interesting; and I shall refer the patient to Dr. Lillienthal.

There is nothing more lamentable than such a case as this. There is nothing so affecting as to see a case which is almost hopeless. That child is but little above an idiot. It can see and hear, but cannot comprehend. It seems, however, to be physically strong. In cases like this we must give an extremely guarded prognosis. No doubt there are institutions and courses of treatment, existing at the present day, whereby such a condition may be relieved. This child cannot talk; scarcely knows how to swallow, and probably would not swallow, if it were not a partially involuntary act.

Surgical Clinic of January 9th, 1875.

Prof. Helmuth [holding up a probe]: Small as this instrument is, and insignificant as it appears to the eye, in the hands of surgeons who understand their business, and who have an educated touch, it becomes of great diagnostic value. It assists us in forming diagnoses, which otherwise might be impossible. It will tell us the direction of a fistula, or the course of a wound; it will tell where a bone is diseased, and what is the condition of the tissues about a wound, whether soft or hard. In many other ways this little instrument renders such service that it cannot be dispensed with by either physician or surgeon.

The exploring trocar is of great value for diagnosing the contents of cavities or tumors, and should be in every pocket-case.

Hip-Joint Disease.

Philip Bound, *Aged Five Years.*

History of Case.—Fell down stairs two months ago; on Christmas day his father hung him up by the feet; since then he has had a great deal of pain, and has not been able to walk.

Prof. Helmuth:

The left hip is affected. You will notice that the gluteal fold is lost on the affected side. There is a distinct line on one side, but it is entirely gone on the other; one side is flattened, and the other appears to be bulging. You will find, I think, that his legs are of different lengths. He has had a great deal of pain since Christmas.

We have had an opportunity during these clinics of seeing hip diseases in very many of its stages; and I am glad to bring this child before you that you may see a case in its second stage. This case exactly illustrates the point that I wish to bring to your notice. I can make a great deal of traction on this leg, and pull with a great deal of force, without increasing the suffering; you see it diminishes it rather than otherwise. Bear in mind that a majority of the children that are affected with hip disease are those having robust constitutions. The old-fashioned idea that hip disease was a strumous or scrofulous irritation of the joint is no longer held. Those who have had the most experience in the treatment of these diseases state, as a fact, that you can generally trace them—in eight cases out of ten—to traumatic origin—to an injury of some kind. This patient three months ago, fell down stairs and injured his hip. If he had been put immediately to bed, and kept quiet, he would have recovered. As it was, the result is entirely different. The boy was allowed to run. The parents did not understand the nature of the disease; and the child was no doubt complaining, from time to time, of the injury. Then came a second injury; and an acute inflammatory action set up between the head of the bone and its socket, the small blood blister or bruise that existed at the head of the femur became still more inflamed, and the consequence is, that we have the second stage of hip disease coming on, with a tendency to effusion, which gives him excessive pain (which is worse at night), and causes an apparent elongation of the limb. Suppuration may follow the inflammatory process; an abscess may form and open on the outside; and that may be followed by caries of the bone.

Hip-Joint Disease.

August Sissman, *Aged Twelve Years.*

(*Continued from page* 60, 85, *and* 105.)

You recollect how emaciated this boy looked when he first came here, how sick he appeared, and how painful it was to move him. He had hip disease in the third stage. I put on him a Bauer's splint, because it was the least expensive; and was preferable to those secured by plaster, because the latter sometimes slip. The object of the extension apparatus is to keep up traction sufficient to draw the head of the bone from the cavity, and allow the body sufficient motion to enable the patient by exercise to keep up the general health. In many cases of hip disease the patient is placed in the recumbent posture, and a weight is applied to the foot. But during such treatment the constitution suffers so much from the confinement, that the object we are attempting to accomplish is often thwarted. This boy has improved very much under the treatment. He states that he has a good appetite; and you see that the roses are coming to his cheeks again. He then had a hectic flush; now he has the tint of health. One of the openings in his hip is nearly closed, while the other is getting better. He has been taking silicea—30th. Continue giving him the same medicine, and bring him back to-day three weeks. I think that I can say that by May you will have him pretty well cured, unless he gets a cold; I mean that the abscesses will heal, and the boy will be comparatively comfortable. He will limp a little for a considerable time.

Angular Curvature of the Spine.

(*Continued from page* 41.)

(*No name given.*)

You will recollect that this child had Potts' disease of the spine. She has been under treatment since October 1. We think that she is better; she certainly is no worse. Even if the child were to grow up with that slight protuberance on her back, it would scarcely be noticed. She has been taking cal. carb., 30th. Continue it and bring her back in four weeks. We shall then see a more visible improvement.

Prof. Helmuth quizzes the class:

Q. What do you understand by tumor, surgically speaking? A. The term is restricted to an enlargement of part or structure caused by some specific morbid growth.

Q. What are some of the diagnostic differences between an innocent and a malignant tumor?

INNOCENT.	MALIGNANT.
1. Harmless with reference to the surrounding structures.	1. The tumor is apt to destroy or involve surrounding structures.
2. Texture bears some resemblance to certain of the surrounding structures.	2. Texture differs from the normal structure of the human body.
3. Non-liability to return (excepting recurrent fibroid.)	3. Great disposition to return.
4. Absence of hemorrhage.	4. Liability to profuse bleeding.
5. Little disposition to soften.	5. Great tendency to soften.
6. Not much tendency to ulcerate.	6. Great tendency to ulceration.
7. Rarely accompanied by offensive discharges.	7. Very offensive, ichorous or bloody discharge.
8. Non-infiltration of surrounding structures.	8. Infiltration of the parts on which they grow, which is often entirely transformed.

Q. What is the color of tumors? A. They vary with the number of blood-vessels contained in them, and also with the amount of inflammatory action in the tumor, or in the superimposed tissue.

Q. What is the color of nævus? A. Purple.

Q. Of fatty tumors? A. Yellow.

Q. Fibrous tumors? A. Whitish.

Q. Cartilaginous tumors? A. White and glistening.

Q. What is the consistency of fibrous and scirrhous tumors? A. Hard.

Q. What of cystic tumors? A. Soft.

Q. What is a hypertrophic tumor? A. Is one which consists of an enlargement or increase of the proper tissue of the part; sometimes having a distinct capsule, and contained in the substance of an organ.

Q. What glands are mostly attacked? A. Especially the tonsils and the prostate, meibomian, thyroid, and mammary glands.

Q. What is the simplest variety? A. Chronic enlargement of the tonsils.

Q. What are fibro-cystic tumors? A. Those in which cysts form in fibrous tumors, either by an accumulation of fluid in the insterstices or by local softening with serous effusion.

Q. What are recurring fibroid tumors, and on what part of the body do they grow? A. They are soft, fragile, lobulated tumors, of fibrous structure, grow on the fingers, within glands, and in the jaw in close proximity to the bone.

Q. How can you distinguish abscess from aneurism? A. By the absence of the thrill, by the fluctuation, and previous history of the case.

Q. Which is the most malignant and fatal variety of cancerous growth? A. The encephaloid cancer.

Q. What is diffuse aneurism? A. It is formed by the blood escaping from a wound in an artery, into the surrounding cellular texture.

Q. What arteries are most liable to aneurism? A. The aorta and popliteal artery.

Q. What are the diagnostic signs between an abscess and an aneurism?

A. From the earliest stage of abscess the tumor is hot, throbbing, hard, and incompressible; in aneurism the tumor is of natural temperature, and is soft and fluctuating.

The skin covering an abscess is inflamed and discolored; that which covers an aneurism is of natural color, or perhaps paler.

In abscess the formation of the tumor is much more rapid than in aneurism.

In aneurism the tumor is pulsating; in abscess it is fluctuating.

Abscesses which lie directly over arteries are lifted up every time the blood is driven along under them, and hence they pulsate like aneurisms; but they do not pulsate when small, whereas aneurisms do from the beginning of their growth. Aneurisms are soft at first, and hard afterwards; whereas abscesses are generally hard at first, and finally soft.

The enlargement in abscess cannot be diminished by pressure; in aneurism the contrary is the case.

(From Prof. Helmuth's work on Surgery.)

The following is recorded of Dr. Dease, of Dublin: "He was called to see a case, supposed to be one of aneurism by all the physicians who had attended it, and, upon careful examination, determined it to be a large collection of pus, overlying an artery. Taking the responsibility, in spite of the advice of those who consulted with him, he plunged his knife into the pulsating mass. There was a gush of matter, and the patient, who looked a short time before upon his case as hopeless, was entirely relieved. Much credit was justly the meed of Dr. Dease, and great gratification must he have felt at thus relieving the unfortunate sufferer. Some time after, he was sent for to another case, which, like that just mentioned, had been regarded as an aneurism; and, as in the other, he decided that it was a collection of pus, and proposed relief in the same manner. This being assented to, he penetrated the tumor with his knife, when out rushed a torrent of blood, and with it the life of the patient. He had erred in his diagnosis. It was an aneurism—not an abscess! Dr. Dease returned to his home, and on the next morning was found upon the floor of his chamber with his throat cut from ear to ear, by his own hand!"

Surgical Clinic of January 16th, 1875.

Cold Abscess.

HARRY PICKARD, *Aged Five Years.*

(*Continued from page* 113.)

PROF. HELMUTH:

On the side of this little boy's jaw you will recollect that there was a hard substance we thought indicated the formation of a cold abscess. There is a great deal of difference in the formation of pus, when inflammatory action seems to exist, and when there is none that is apparent. In fact, a large accumulation of pus can take place in a cavity of the body, and yet its formation be unattended by the usual symptoms which belong to acute inflammation; but, on the contrary, the system will be seriously affected by the symptoms which indicate constitutional irritation. You can have the formation of a large quantity of pus taking place in the body, or some occult spot and yet have none of those inflammatory symptoms which belong to acute forms of suppuration. Instead of having a high degree of inflammatory action, we may have a low, broken-down condition of the system —irritability, quick pulse, pale face, loss of appetite—and a general condition of the whole body indicating that there is a great deal of irritation; and we may even find hectic fever, resulting in regular chills, which may be mistaken, on account of the regularity of the paroxysms, for intermittent fever.

This is a simple case of cold abscess on the side of the cheek. There is nothing more difficult to diagnose than a cold abscess—that is to say, a chronic abscess—when there is a large quantity of matter involved. There are some pressure symptoms in abscesses, which are of a most perplexing nature. Small as this abscess appears, it offers a fruitful subject for a lecture; but we have been over the subject quite fully, and I will only refer to the insidious nature of those abscesses which occur in different parts of the body—and especially in cavities where the pressure symptoms give rise to a great many obscure symptoms.

Spermatorrhœa.

GEORGE W. FLEMING, *Aged Thirty Years.*

The patient, who has brought a card of introduction to me, states that he has been told that he has some trouble with the prostate gland; has had symptoms of the disease for twelve years. After every stool, or the passage of urine, there is a discharge of a dirty, yellowish-white fluid from the urethra—about a thimblefull in quantity. Can remain all day and all night without urinating.

Q. The chief symptom that you have now is the loss of some fluid after you pass water. Does that, and its train of symptoms, make you feel badly, and weak at times? A. I cannot say that it makes me feel badly.

Q. Does it worry your mind? A. No, sir.

Q. Does it make you feel weak, or give you any pain in the loins, or humming in the ear? A. No.

Q. You only desire to get rid of it, because of its unpleasantness? A. That is the reason; and because I thought it might become worse after a while.

Q. Have you, in addition to this discharge, a loss of power? A. Yes; for the last four or five months.

Q. Do you have any desire for sexual connection, or does the loss of desire and of power go together? A. I have no desire at all now.

Q. Does this discharge pass from you without any excitement? A. Yes.

Taking the age of the patient into consideration, the probability is against there being a disease of the prostate gland, unless it be some disease of traumatic origin. You do not generally find disease of the prostate gland until forty-five or fifty years have passed. The enlargement of the prostate is, as Sir Henry Thompson says, the common heritage of mankind. Nine-tenths of the men (I except women) as they advance to the age of fifty or sixty, have more or less enlargement of the prostate gland. I do not know whether any of you have ever tried to dissect the prostate gland from the bladder; but if you should, you will find it very difficult to discover where the prostate begins and where the bladder ends. One seems to run directly into the other. The prostate seems almost to be a continuation of the bladder.

There is something else the matter with this gentleman. He has not an enlargement of the prostate, but he has, I think, a relaxation of the ejaculatory ducts. These ducts open on each side of the verumontanum. I will first examine the rectum. I feel the prostate gland distinctly. The better way in such an examination is to put the patient on his side, introduce the finger and turn the ball of the finger up, because that is the most sensitive part. As I pass the finger along, I can feel his prostate gland. It is quite soft and flexible, and has not that stony hardness which belongs to certain forms of disease. I will now pass a catheter into the bladder. In doing this it is important, in the first place, that you select a catheter having the proper curve. If the man had a prostatic enlargement, this sound would not begin to pass the entrance. You would have to take one the arc of whose circle was at least an inch longer. The curve would have to be greater to carry the end of the instrument over the prostate gland; but finding that the gland is not enlarged, I am quite sure that this catheter will enter. You place the patient either on his back, or leaning backward against the wall. Have the catheter well oiled, or, what is better, inject a small syringe-full of warm oil into the urethra. I have, on more than one occasion, entered the bladder and relieved men without the introduction of an instrument at all—after they had been tunneled half the night with an instrument—by simply injecting into the bladder a little warm oil. At all events, let the instrument be well oiled; hold it between the finger and thumb of the right hand, the curved part downwards; you can then introduce it in the way I now do it; then bring it up, so that the handle of the instrument is parallel with the abdomen; then draw the penis up, with one hand on the instrument, and depress it between the legs of the patient. Do not use any force in the passage of the catheter. A steady, mild pressure, applied when the catheter meets an obstruction, will generally succeed better than any rough manipulation, because there is no portion of the human body so susceptible to spasmodic action as the urethra. If, in treating spasmodic stric- you fail to enter the bladder the first time, do not try any more that day; because every time an instrument passes along the urethra and touches the part which is irritated, it will cause more violent contractions; and by using force to overcome the obstruction, you may make a false passage, and necessarily render the patient a great deal worse.

This patient has not an enlargement of the prostate gland, but he has a paralysis of the ejaculatory ducts, which open on either side of the veru-montanum. What is the best medicine? At one time there was a great deal of talk about cauterizing, and for this purpose an instrument was used, consisting of a catheter with a cylinder at the extremity of the wire, at the bottom of which cylinder was placed some powdered caustic. You then draw this cylinder within the sheath of the instrument, and having introduced it into the urethra, you push forward the cylinder, and allow it to come in contact with the floor of the urethra. The heat of the body then melts the tallow or pomade, and the caustic drops down. This treatment (Lallemand's) was highly recommended for spermatorrhœa, or for loss of semen. I used it a great many times, but I must say, that I never saw the first shadow of good come from it, and I believe that is the general experience of physicians, if they would speak the truth. The treatment gives rise to a great deal of pain. Sometimes, when the first burning takes place, there may be an arrest of the symptoms, but as a general rule it is not in the end successful. But still it is highly recommended. Another method of treatment is by a pad; and these pads were sold by the quacks by thousands. There is no disease that is discussed in so many yellow-covered books as spermatorrhœa. There is no disease that upsets a man's moral faculties more than a loss of semen or virile power. This loss of semen, whether from spermatorrhœa or masturbation, or from other causes—it makes no difference what—causes patient to become morbid. Although they do not like to own it, they are fearful, and are ready to grasp at any thing that appears to offer relief. They become morose, and desire to hide their condition from other people. They buy these yellow-covered books, which advertise a pad, or somebody's specific; and they shut themselves up in a room and read it, and send a dollar to the publisher to procure a pad, or a prescription, but do not tell anybody what they have done. That is the course that is followed in nine-tenths of such cases; and nobody is any the wiser. The only way that we can judge of the extent to which this business is carried on, is by the fact that all the proprietors of these "specifics" grow rich. There are ten thousand men not far from here, who have these yellow-covered books secreted in a drawer, and a bottle of medicine, or a pad, hidden away where no one can find it—simply because they do not want any one to know that they have this trouble. No one can estimate the amount of money that goes into the pockets of these outrageous quacks; and we can only judge of the amount by the fine mansions and equipages they are able to support.

As I have already said, I do not regard the caustic treatment as of much value, and I have given it, I think, a fair trial. But there are several medicines that will relieve this condition—such as phosphorous, phosphoric acid, opium, and picric acid. We will give him picric acid, 3rd—four doses per day; and every night let him sit for five or ten minutes in a basin of cold water in which has been dissolved two handfuls of salt. After taking the bath the parts are to be thoroughly rubbed. Take the medicine for two weeks, and then come back. I have never used picric acid, but it has the reputation of having cured some remarkable cases. We will give it a trial in this case to see how it acts.

Enlargement of the Salivary Glands.

LIZZIE SMITH, *Aged Eighteen Years.*

A Lump on her Throat.—Digestion begins in the mouth, in mastication and the admixture of the food with those substances which come from the salivary glands. We have the parotid glands, the submaxillary, the sublingual, and the intralingual, emptying the saliva into the laced cavity. The parotid gland pours out three-fourths of all the saliva that we use. This gland sometimes becomes diseased; and in some instances is affected with an enlargement called the mumps. The submaxillary gland lies lower down, on the inner side of the inferior maxillary bone. All of these glands are under the influence of the nervous system, and they can pour out into the mouth their secretions by a nervous act. For instance, if, when you were a boy, hungry and poor, you gazed into the window of a cake shop, the saliva would flow into your mouth; that is what is called "mouth-watering." It is by the nervous action on the glands that they are stimulated to secretion. These glands, which secrete the salivia, sometimes enlarge. There are other diseases which are specific in their character which I will not now describe. An enlargement of the salivary glands, with a tendency to suppuration, can be entirely cured by the use of mercury. I hope that this will not suppurate, although it now presents many inflammatory symptoms. When you have a salivary gland which is enlarged and hard, and there is an increase in the flow of saliva, then, of course, mercurius is the medicine, because mercurius, taken by a healthy person, will cause an enlargement of the glands and increase the flow of saliva. In other cases, where there is an enlargement, but no increased flow of saliva, belladonna is the remedy. Other medicines are baryta. carb., conium., sulph. etc.

Surgical Clinic of January 23rd, 1875.

Prof. Helmuth being called suddenly to Stamford, Dr. Thompson, after reading a letter explaining the absence of the Professor, conducted the Clinic.

False Anchylosis.

LUCY FRANCIS, *Aged Five Years.*

DR. J. H. THOMPSON:

This is a case sent by Prof. S. P. Burdick. In July last she fell down and broke her arm at the elbow. It has been broken three times, and the elbow-joint is quite stiff. The second breaking of the arm was done by a physician, because it had been improperly set. This is the first that I have seen of the case. The physician put splints on, and kept them on for three weeks. When the splints were taken off he could not move the arm. Three weeks is an uncommonly short time for an arm to become stiff in a child; but it is not too long to keep the splints on, in ordinary cases. The only way that I can account for this arm becoming stiff in that time, is by assuming that there might have been a fracture of the condyle, and an effusion thrown out; in that case it might have become anchylosed in that time. I think that you could get some movement in this joint, if passive motion was persisted in. It would be well to put the patient under the influence of an anæsthetic, and have those adhesions broken up. Unless this is done soon, she will have a stiff arm as long as she lives. Passive motion is the only manner of cure and of preserving the joint, after a fracture at, or near the joint; and it must be persisted in perseveringly, but without using too much force. If you use too much violence in producing this passive motion, you do a great deal more harm than good. Therefore, to be beneficial, it must be persisted in for a long time, but not to such an extent as to throw the patient into a fever each time, as was done in this case. You will remember the case of the little boy, at the first Clinic of this season, whose arm was fractured at the external condyle. He came to my office a great many times after that, and I made passive motion with the arm with the utmost care; but I have not succeeded in getting a perfect motion of the joint, and the motion is still somewhat impeded. So you will observe that it is not always a means of perfect restoration, even when properly attended to. In this case, perhaps, the passive motion was carried to too great an extent, and stiffness of the muscle, instead of flexibility, was the result. But the only chance of obtaining a movable joint is to place the patient under the influence of ether, break up these adhesions, and then carefully persist in passive motion for three or four weeks.

Encysted Tumor.

TIMOTHY DARLY, *Aged Forty-two Years.*

History of Case.—The patient states tha the has had this on his back for about twenty years; has another smaller one near it which has been there for twenty-five years. The large one was lanced about a year ago and then healed up. It did not trouble the patient much until then. It broke this morning. Before it broke it was smooth and round.

DR. J. H. THOMPSON:

This is an encysted tumor. They will sometimes remain without much increase in size or occasioning inconvenience for a long time. About a year ago suppurative action set up in this tumor, and pus probably found its way to the surface, just within the membrane of the sac, under the skin. It was then lanced, and soon afterwards healed up. Since that time, suppuration has again taken place; and this morning the tissues became so thin that the sac ruptured. As I squeeze it you see all the contents of the tumor gush out. There is some pus mixed with it. The suppuration has probably destroyed the sac, and we will apply strips of adhesive plaster, and I think very likely that adhesion may take place, and a spontaneous cure result without any operative interference.

Hydrocele.

GEORGE CAMPION, *Aged Fifty-two Years.*

This is a hydrocele. I saw this patient in the dispensary on Tuesday, and requested him to come to my house that night, when I injected the compound tincture of iodine into the sac, without drawing off any of the serum. About two hours after I had done this, there was considerable inflammation set up, which continued until last night. On Thursday he called again to see me. The treatment which I adopted is a new one. The case is going on now very well, and I shall not do any thing further. I simply brought him here to-day to show you the result of the treatment.

Abscess.

HENRY TURNHERR, *Aged Twenty-eight Years.*

An abscess is forming in the lower jaw. The patient states that it resulted from a blow. Let it be poulticed every three hours, and let the patient return on Tuesday.

Varicose Ulcer.

MARY KEGAN, *Aged Thirty-two Years.*

I have brought this case to show you a varicose ulcer. This patient is a washerwoman, and stands on her feet a great deal. Varicose ulcers are frequent with such people. The blood passes down the limbs, the coats of the veins become dilated, so that the valves cannot perform their functions properly, the blood does not return freely, and you have congestion. Here you see the varicose veins. The foot is very much enlarged. The circulation becomes impeded, and finally an ulcer forms. She has been in this condition for twelve or fifteen years; she has had this open sore for nine or ten years. It has occasionally healed up to within about a pin's head, and then it would break out again; as the inflammation increased, the sore would gradually extend, until it finally got into the condition in which you now see it. By keeping her foot upon a chair for a while, and stopping work, it would partly heal up. The pain is always worse at night.

The best treatment for this, in the first place, is rest; but, as this disease generally appears in persons who cannot rest, it continues until it assumes the form you now see. If this patient could go to bed and keep the horizontal position for two or three months, this leg would get well. The palliative treatment, which is almost the only one you can use in this case, is to bandage the leg, or apply an elastic stocking. The elastic stocking is very valuable in such cases, as it keeps up a constant pressure on the foot or leg. It must be tighter below than it is above; because, if you have it tight above and loose below, you will have a worse constriction than with the leg unbandaged. The radical cure is effected by the destruction of the vein with caustic potash or acupressure. I would recommend the patient, besides bandaging the limb, to apply to the sore an ointment, composed of Red Precipitate of Mercury, 1 drachm; Simple Cerate, 1 ounce. Spread on a piece of linen. Dress the limb twice a day. By this treatment she can continue her occupation, and the limb may become very much improved.

Lipoma Nasi.

MARY GAAS, *Aged Thirty-six Years.*

This patient has an ulcerated condition of the palatine portion of the mouth, in addition to lipoma of the nose. Lipoma comes in two forms—flattened and pedunculated. When pedunculated, it sometimes hangs down on the face to an extent of several inches. It occurs more frequently in man than in woman; and generally in men who are over fifty years of age, and who have been addicted to high living, or to the use of alcoholic beverages. I do not know of any remedy that can be given internally that will have much effect upon this disease. The knife is the only resort, and that is better resorted to in cases where the lipoma is pedunculated than where it is flattened. This disease never interferes with the mucous structure or with the cartilage of the nose. Although it is with a great deal of difficulty that it can be removed, yet with care it can be done. I shall not undertake to operate upon this case to-day, because there is so much surface involved that I am afraid that we should not find material enough to make the flaps to cover the gap. If there should be any thing specific in the case, of which we have some indication in the pharynx, we should have a more unhappy result than if we left it in its present condition. It has been recommended by some that iodine should be employed locally; and I will use it in this case. But, instead of applying the tincture of iodine, which would give her a great deal of pain, I will prescribe an ointment of the iodide of potash. The prescription is thus written:

"℞: Ung. Potas. Iod. ℥ij."

Spread the ointment on a piece of linen and apply it to the nose.

Periostitis.

Bridget Doyle, *Aged Twenty-three Years.*

History of Case.—A felon on the end of the index finger of left hand. Has been sore three weeks. Does not remember bruising it in any way. She poulticed it for a while, and then opened it with a needle. It then became worse, and she went to a doctor, and had it opened with a knife, but not very deep.

Dr. Thompson:

This, as you know, is a form of felon—the fourth variety in which the pus forms under the periosteum; and in this case the bone has become diseased. In treating this disease where the inflammation has affected the deep tissues, and there has been an effusion of pus under the periosteum, slight incisions do more harm than good. You must go down into and through the periosteum, to allow of the evacuation of pus underneath; for that is the cause of all the trouble. If you prick it lightly through the skin, you may perhaps find a little pus, which has formed under that tissue, but the discharge of that will give relief for only a few hours. If you wish to do the patient a real service and give permanent relief, you must cut down until you feel the bone with the point of the knife. If the patient had gone to a doctor in time, and had the finger thus opened, I have no doubt she would have saved the bone, which I now feel with the probe and easily remove. The end of the finger should be tightly bandaged every day, and the openings will soon heal.

Partial Paralysis of the Œsophagus.

SIDNEY FANNING, *Aged Fifty-five Years.*

The patient states: I was sent here by Dr. Rushmore, of Hempstead. My trouble is in my throat, above the entrance to the wind-pipe. It has been coming on for a year or more; but more rapidly within the last four or six months. I have very great pain in swallowing, and frequent coughing. Dr. Rushmore said that it was an obscure case, and sent me here to find out what was the matter. After talking a little while, it hurts me. In eating, if I use soft food, the most of it will pass down. If I use hard foods it will remain in the throat. I make every effort to swallow, but it remains, and I can eject it, as I would phlegm. It seems sometimes almost impossible for me to swallow any hard food. I can exercise but very little. I gave out twice in coming up these stairs. The pain is only in the act of swallowing. I have no difficulty in breathing. At times it is very difficult for me to make any effort to swallow; and I will go for hours without even swallowing spittle. I can drink warm fluids, if they are not too warm, better than cold.

Dr. Thompson:

I will refer this case to Dr. Houghton who will examine his throat with a laryngoscope.

Abscess.

John Thomas, *Aged Twenty-three Years.*

Dr. J. H. Thompson:

This patient was sent to my house on Thursday by Dr. Norton, suffering with an abscess just back of the anus. The skin over it was very thin, indeed, and I opened it and evacuated a large quantity of pus. I told him to poultice it, and he has done so, and took the poultice off this morning. This may be the beginning of a fistula. It was a very large abscess when I opened it. It does not hurt him at all now. I gave him Silicea, 30th trituration, internally, three times a day. He need not poultice it any more, but may continue the use of the silicea for a short time longer.

Surgical Clinic of January 30th, 1875.

Cleft Palate.

MISS VAN HOUGHTON.

(*Continued from page* 55.)

PROF. HELMUTH :

Gentlemen: You recollect I presented to you a case of cleft palate early in the session, and you remember I stated at the time, that this class of cases was hardly the variety to operate upon before you, because it would be impossible for you to see the steps of the operation, which is always tedious. This patient was therefore removed to the surgical hospital, and the operation was performed with instruments with long handles, such as you see here. This was the operation: I pared the edges of the fissure; Dr. Thompson put in the stitches, and Dr. Cranch took them out. It is always proper and necessary that you have instruments with long handles, and particularly that the knives shall have long shanks, and a short cutting edge. You should also have blades bent at right angles, to loosen the tissue from the palatine bones, and also a double-edged knife to insert under the edge of the palate, to divide the levator palati, in order that the flaps may fall together after you have pared them. Then you have scissors, with handles such as you see here, and a long needle-holder. The needles you use are the same as those for vesico vaginal fistula, sharp and round, with no cutting edge. They should be threaded with silk, and the wire hooked into that. Here is one of them, round, and curved at the end. If you have a long needle, it is almost impossible to draw it through one lip of the cleft, before you introduce it into the other. Now, holding the needle at an angle, you introduce it on one side about a quarter of an inch from the margin, and you push it through and catch it inside the cleft, draw it out, and draw the silk through. Then enter it on the other side, directly opposite, and draw it through. It is better to put in two or three stitches at once, before you draw them together. If the case is a very severe one, as now shown you, you will have to perform two, and perhaps three operations. So far, this has been a successful operation, and, as you see, I prefer to bring in the patient after its performance, that you may observe for yourselves, rather than to keep you sitting in the amphitheatre while the operation is going on. This would be tedious, you could see nothing and could learn nothing. [To the patient: Open your mouth.] You can see the cleft is almost closed. There still remains an opening at the roof of the mouth. [The surgeon introduces a spatula into the patient's mouth.] Now you can view it very well, by looking at the roof of the mouth when the patient holds the head up. It is very nicely united, indeed. You observe the fissure is all closed except a little slit in the upper part of the mouth. The next operation for me to perform will be to close the top of the fissure, and, I hope, the effort will be successful. The stitches were allowed to remain five days before they were taken out.

Phlebolithes.

PROF. HELMUTH:

I will now introduce to you Mr. Howell, who appears before you out of regard for the class, to show you a very peculiar and aggravated case of varicose veins of the right fore-arm.

Q. What is varix? A. Preternatural enlargement of the veins.

HISTORY OF THE CASE BY THE PATIENT.

This condition was discovered when I was about a year old. It didn't bother me any. I had the full use of my arm.

PROF. HELMUTH:

Q. This is a true case of varicose veins. These have existed since birth, have they not? A. Yes, sir. The arm was examined by Prof. Parker, of the Old School, when I was about 7, 8, or 9 years old. I could not stand the pressure he recommended.

Q. You never had any hemorrhage from them? A. No, sir.

Q. Do they give you much pain? A. No; unless I am unwell; then I feel pain. What I want to call your attention to is, you will feel all the way down the arms hard, bony deposits.

By PROF. HELMUTH:

This is a peculiar condition of the veins. After they have become diseased for some time, and their coats seem to have become enlarged, a deposit takes place within them. These concretions are first cartilaginous, but finally an ossific deposit takes place in the coats of the vessels. By taking hold of the arm and pressing upon the larger veins, in the neighborhood of the valves, here and there, you can feel quite distinctly the presence of the foreign substance, which really seems to be bony. In some places it is cartilaginous certainly. Nature is trying to cure the disease. Now, this is simply an illustration of how long a disease may continue and the patient not be obliged to be confined, and also how a formation may exist in the veins themselves, and yet no manifest change be shown from the obstruction of the circulation.

Q. Do you have any numbness in that part? A. No, sir.

Q. Does it hurt you? [Prof. Helmuth presses on the veins.] A. Yes, sir; now it does.

Q. It doesn't interfere with your general health? A. No, not at all; and the more exercise I have the better it is.

Q. You have given up treatment? A. I don't do any thing, except I bathe it almost invariably in the morning with cold water. I have had a good deal of experience with it. I used to carry my arm up, but I noticed it would grow weaker; and when I would lay it down a little, it would instantly pain me. Now I hold it hanging down, and never have any pain.

Q. Do you find the condition increases? A. No; I don't think it does.

Q. I have no doubt those veins will be obliterated if your health continues good. The valves will be shut down, and there will be ossific deposit. The outside ones may rupture, you may have severe hemorrhage, and, as I say, the veins will then become obliterated. This is a trial on the part of Nature to do away with this condition, and she is endeavoring to place obstacles that will obstruct the circulation, and she is doing it now.

Q. Do you find these deposits grow? A. Yes; they are growing—some of them I can feel increasing in size every day.

This is a very rare case, and I am very much obliged to the gentleman for offering us the opportunity of inspecting it. In the ordinary treatment of varix there are a great many methods employed for the relief of the enlargement. By the application of caustic lime and soda, an eschar is produced. Another method is the passage of two pins underneath the veins, winding over them a silk suture to obstruct the circulation, then introducing a tenotome, and dividing the veins between the pins. For instance, we have veins that are tortuous. We introduce a pin underneath the vein and bring it out there, and (illustrating on black-board) another pin there. Then we twist over the pins a figure 8 suture of silk; then pass the tenotome underneath the veins flatways, turn up the edge, and cut it through. This is one of the very best methods of obliteration.

THE PATIENT: Do you think there is more than one vein implicated here?

PROF. HELMUTH: Oh, yes; I think all the superficial veins of the fore-arm are involved.

Onychia Maligna.

WM. BROWN, *Aged Five Years.*

PROF. HELMUTH:

Here is a patient who has disease of the toe-nail which has become inverted. The nail is dead, and it will be necessary to remove it, and I will now proceed to do so. The patient is a little boy. Put him on the bed; let his foot hang down over the end, that we may see the condition of the nail. It is dead, putrid—black; but still it lies in the matrix, and there yet remains enough connection between the dead and living structure, to keep up a certain amount of unhealthy growth. The nail must be removed at its root. This is a different affection from the ordinary ingrowing toe-nail; in the one case the nail grows in and obstructs the circulation, and we have ulceration as from a foreign body. In this case, however, the disease is at the root of the nail itself. You see it smells like a piece of dead bone, and must be removed as soon as possible; and we will therefore spray it with ether and produce local anæsthesia. Before the introduction of local anæsthesia, we often used to freeze portions of the body before operating upon them, and in this way I have removed many tumors. The preparation principally used in those days was ice and salt. Then came ether, and then local anæsthesia, as it is now used for many surgical operations, such as lancing a felon, the removal of small tumors, portions of toe-nail, etc. But there is a substance which readily chills the tissue to insensibility, and that is Rhigolene, introduced by Henry J. Bigelow, M. D., of Boston. It takes about three minutes to freeze the parts. [Prof. Helmuth extracts the nail.] You see that, although the top of the nail was in a very diseased condition, still at its root it was quite healthy, there being sufficient action going on from the matrix to keep up a certain amount of healthy nutrition. The removal of nails is very painful, and the trouble arising afterwards is, that there is a tendency to the formation of unhealthy granulations, which ultimately result in a fungous growth. I will first stop the hemorrhage by pressure, as there will be considerable. I will then apply a plaster of oxide of zinc; watch the parts very closely, and, if the granulations seem to be unhealthy, we will give nitric acid internally, and apply a solution to the parts.

Let me explain to you a little how these nails grow.

You all know that we have the skin divided into *two* layers, the cutis vera, or the true skin, being the inferior layer. It is composed of two layers, the corium and papillary body, and over the papillæ lies the basement membrane, and then the epiderma. The office of the former is to generate cells, which, as they come to the surface, become scales and are cast off. The epidermis and the corium are reflected back on each finger, as you see there, and a groove is formed and the papillary body comes up to the groove. From the papillary body we have the basement membrane, and new cells are formed from the basement membrane, and this constitutes the matrix of the nail. The cell is formed in the groove of the epiderma, and the nail grows out as you see there. Now, in removing the toe-nail, you seize it with forceps and withdraw it by force; but sometimes the granulations are so unhealthy, and there seems to be so much constitutional irritation, and the parts have become so exceedingly sensitive, that you have to use not only local, but general anæsthesia. Often in very aggravated cases of ingrowing toe-nail, you can cure your patient by taking a knife, holding it as if you were about to whittle, and, shaving off the tissues straight down to the nail, letting the nail remain as it is. Another excellent method is to scrape the nail on the top until it becomes sensitive, cut a notch into the centre of the apex of it, and elevate each side by tucking under it lead, such as you will find in tea boxes. Another method was contrived by a dentist, and is one not generally known. He simply bent a little piece of silver wire into a curved shape, and turned in each end like a hook. He raised up the ends of thé nail and hooked the ends of this spring under them, and the constant traction of the spring had a tendency to raise the nail from the sides and let it grow out. It is a very nice method, and you can make the instrument yourself. A little piece of watch-spring will answer the same purpose. You can cover it with a piece of thread. It is astonishing how little pressure it takes to cause a nail to grow in the right direction.

Rupture of the Coraco Clavicular Ligament and Bruised Capsular Ligament.

WILLIAM SPELMAN, *Aged Sixty-eight Years.*

Q. Where were you born? A. Philadelphia.

Q. Blackberry alley? A. No, sir; at the corner of Sixth and Lombard streets.

Q. I was your neighbor. Did you know Doctors Helmuth and Sims? You have come to the right place at last? A. I cannot raise this arm.

Q. [To the Students.] Are any of you, gentlemen, prepared to diagnose this case—you who are looking for those glossy sheepskins? We have been lecturing a good deal of late on shoulder affections, and this will be quite interesting.

Q. [To the Patient.] Now tell me about your trouble. Stand face to face. Does that hurt you (moving arm upward)? A. It pains.

Q. Where does it pain you? A. Under my shoulder.

Q. Stand straight—put your elbow on your chest—now put your hand up here (on opposite shoulder). He has now his elbow down to his chest and his hand on the opposite side. Now we will see what else is the matter. I will examine his shoulders from behind. There is a little difference in their contour, the uninjured one being a little higher. Put your hand behind you—

the affected hand. Bend it at the elbow. Bend it up this way (to a right angle). Does it hurt you any? A. Yes.

Q. Where does it hurt you? A. There (at the joint).

Q. Now, put it forward again. Now, put your hand up to the top of your head. A. I cannot do that.

Q. Let me see how high you can raise it. A. This won't let me get it up (putting his hand to acromion).

Q. What won't? A. The pain there.

Q. Does it hurt you very much? A. It does.

Q. Right where I have my fingers, all around the head of that bone? A. Yes.

Q. You may turn around; does it hurt you there, too? A. Yes, sir, very much.

Q. Now, tell me how you fell? A. My foot slipped.

Q. Then, did you fall? A. Right down on my shoulder.

Q. But you can't get your hand to your head? A. No, sir. It is not broken, but it is bruised, and I want to know what I can do for it.

Q. We have looked for these three things. First, we have got rid of the dislocation into the axilla, but he cannot raise his hand to the top of his head, and he cannot put his hand in *this* direction, (upward), but can put it so (downward). He has all the muscular actions of his fore-arm. I cannot find that he has any fracture, but he has certainly bruised the capsular ligament, and it will be a long time before he recovers; and at the same time he has also ruptured the ligament that holds the clavicle on the top of the shoulder joint; that is quite evident; you can feel the end of the bone under the finger. [To the patient.] You will get over this, but it will take a long time. A. That is what I think myself.

Q. Then you agree with me in my diagnosis? A. Yes, sir!

Q. That is all right. The best remedy is to keep the arm well supported at the elbow with a sling, and to hold it across the chest in that manner. Bathe the parts thoroughly with a solution of arnica and water. Let it rest. We will have a sling made for you, and it will get along. You will have to hold your elbow right up so. Come and see us in about two weeks. I presume this is your first introduction to the medical profession? A. I have never had a doctor before.

Prof. Helmuth: That is the reason why you have lived so long.

Q. [To the Students.] What is the difference between this

injury and fracture of the surgical neck of the humerus? A. If it were a fracture, raising the arm at the shoulder would restore shape to the parts.

Q. When you push up the head of the bone from the elbow, in fracture of the humerus, and let go of it, how would it be; would it remain there, or drop down? A. Drop down.

Q. In fracture of the surgical neck of the humerus, then, how would a patient look when he came for treatment; how would the shoulder be, when you looked at him from behind? A. The shoulder would be dropped like that.

Q. This man has very little dropping of the shoulder. In the fracture of the surgical neck of the humerus, the affected shoulder is flattened?

Movable Cartilage.

Mr. Fisk, *Aged Forty Years.*

Q. Can you give us a little history of this trouble? A. The first symptom I noticed was quite a sudden pain in the knee, like a bruise, which for three or four weeks troubled me very much. I looked at my knee, but could see nothing—no bruising, or any thing of that kind. I then examined underneath to the right, and between the cords I found a lump about the size of a walnut, and it has grown larger until it has grown to be about half the size of an egg. I used to bandage it, for it goes back sometimes, and cannot be felt, but it pains me.

Q. What is your business? A. A carpenter.

Q. Are you on your feet a great deal? A. Yes, sir.

Q. Did you sprain that knee or fall down. A. No, sir; never to my knowledge.

Q. Let us see it. [Prof. Helmuth examines the popliteal space.] Does this ever give you any sudden pain? A. I will sit down to my dinner, get up, and be lame from it, and have to limp. [Patient gets on the table.]

Q. Does it disappear on pressure? A. Below there, it does sometimes.

Q. We will now compare legs. Can you get the tumor out when you want to? A. It will come out when I come down on my feet (getting off the table).

Q. Does the pain come suddenly? A. No, sir.

Q. Does it catch you? A. No, sir.

Q. It is hard to the touch? A. No, sir; soft.

Q. Judging from the character of this disease, and from the manner this tumor appears and disappears, the sudden character of the pain, and the stiffness of the joint when he attempts to move, I should say, perhaps, there is a loose cartilage within the joint. There are in the cavity of the joints, and more especially in the knee-joint, movable cartilages, which wander from place to place. They seem to originate from the synovial membrane by the side of the joint, and are generally attached to it by a pedicle until some motion of the patient has a tendency to loosen them, and then they move within the joint. There is a good deal of surface between several bones which enter into the formation of the knee, and a cartilage of no very ordinary size—even that of a marble—will move about from place to place, and give rise to little inconvenience except when it comes between the condyles of the femur and the head of the tibia, and pressure is made on it; then the pain is sudden, and the patient even sinks down. The peculiarity of these cartilages, when you come to examine them, is simply this: They bear a close resemblance to healthy cartilage, and perhaps the same relation as the sesamoid bones to the bony portions of the body. They seem to be developed in the joint and grow from the synovial membranes. They are pedunculated at first, and afterwards become loose, and fall in the cavity of the joint. There are several methods which have been recommended for the relief of this affection, and I know one case which was cured entirely, or said to be, by the internal use of rhus. I also gave rhus to a member of the class, a patient, but I don't know that it produced much effect. I know, however, of a patient that was cured through internal administration of medicine. If drugs do not effect a cure, the removal of the offending substance may be effected, by having a strong iron ring made to press down over the cartilage, and making an incision through the diameter of the ring, at the same time pressing on the parts and allowing the foreign substance to pop out; the object being chiefly to prevent air from entering the joint. We will therefore prescribe for this patient for the present.

[To the Patient.] I would like to see you back here in a couple of weeks.

Q. When walking with apparent ease, do you have a sudden pain in the joint? A. A sudden, sharp, sticking pain; a stitch.

Q. But you can move about without much pain? A. Yes, sir.

Q. When you are walking without pain, does this catch you suddenly? A. Yes, sir.

Q. That is the character of these affections. The patient may be walking without pain, and all at once the cartilage falls in between the two portions of the articulation, and the pain is excruciating, the offending material being caught between the bones.

Hip-Joint Disease.

AUGUST SISSMAN, *Aged Twelve Years.*

(*Continued from pages* 60, 85, 105, *and* 116.)

PROF. HELMUTH:

Q. This is the boy that was wearing the splint. I see [to the boy's father] you have bought him a new pair of shoes. How is he now? A. He is pretty good. I bought them because it was bad weather. They are a little larger than the other ones. He has more room in them, and he steps out pretty well.

Q. How are the discharges from his hip? A. Very much better; they come out a great deal less.

Q. Are the discharges less than when you first came? A. Yes, sir.

Q. And he don't have any pain at all? A. No, sir.

Q. His foot now comes down very near to the ground? A. Yes, sir.

Q. Let him walk a little. He steps on it very well, indeed. Do you keep that screwed up (pointing to the bar of the splint)? A. Yes, sir.

Q. Do you take it off at night? A. Yes, sir; in the evening.

Q. [To the Boy.] How do you feel; pretty well? A. Yes, sir.

Q. Aren't you glad you came here? A. Yes, sir; I am.

Q. What medicine is this boy taking? A. Calcarea.

Q. What day did you come here first? A. On November 7th.

In the course of six months this boy I hope will be well, although the leg will always be a little short. But you recollect how he looked the first time. Now he is nearly well.

[Parent.] He goes out every day a couple of hours to stretch his leg; for exercise.

Continue with the medicine. I desire you to bring him here once more, about the last of February, and then we don't want to see him again until next October. I want you to bring him then, as I think by that time he will be nearly cured, and I wish to have him appear before the class.

[To the Students.] One reason that this patient has done so well is because his parents have taken such an interest in his case. In nine, out of every ten such cases, no benefit results, because the treatment is so tedious, and requires such constant watching, that even parents themselves, become negligent in the bestowal of proper attention, such as looking after the splint, giving the limb the requisite amount of rubbing, etc.

Partial Paralysis of the Œsophagus.

SIDNEY FANNING, *Aged Fifty-five Years.*

(*Continued from page* 131.)

[The patient examined with a Laryngoscope.]

PROF. HELMUTH:

This patient will explain his case to you very well, therefore I think I will allow him to tell his story.

The Patient: I judge from the remarks of one of the professors of practice that mine is a case of inflammation of the larynx, and was of such a character, as I understood the doctor to describe Laryngitis Carcinomatous. I forgot the name for three or four days, and was thinking of the word cosmo, but knew that was not it, but I got it afterwards.

Q. What did you say it was? A. Laryngitis Carcinomatous.

Q. What else was there about it? A. Professor Houghton said it was inflammation of the epiglottis as thick as my finger; all the cartilages were enlarged on account of the inflammation. [A student, who was present at the laryngoscopic examination, corrects the patient, and explains the nature of the disease.]

Q. You say there was inflammation all around the perichondrium? A. Yes, sir.

Q. Down to the vocal cord? A. He could not see them very well, but the epiglottis was pressed back and very thick—as thick as my finger.

Q. How long has this been going on; did the doctor prescribe for you? A. He did.

Q. Did you know what he did? A. I could not say.

Q. Now we will find out what the symptoms are. Can you tell us when this trouble first began? A. Ten years ago.

Q. You seem to speak better now than when you first came in; how did it appear first? A. As a hacking at different times. When in church, after singing one or two verses, I always had to go out, and would go this way [coughing]. I remember of that 15 years ago.

Q. Did you become suddenly hoarse; and would you be worse towards evening? A. I don't remember.

Q. Did you have any dryness in your throat, in the morning especially? A. I think I did.

Q. Did you ever lose your voice entirely? A. No, sir.

Q. Does it hurt you to swallow? A. Very much; liquids, or any thing cold, or any thing approaching solids.

Q. Suppose you were to take a warm semi-solid, like milk toast, could you swallow that? A. After swallowing a small portion, and trying a little, then I could gradually swallow soft milk toast.

Q. Do you ever, after swallowing any thing, regurgitate it? A. Not immediately after swallowing. I can swallow part. The other part will remain, and I try to swallow it.

Q. You only get part down? A. Yes, sir.

Q. Do you ever choke when you swallow, and have the fluid come out of your nose? A. Very often; within the last three or four months that has been the trouble with me. Three months ago I could eat pretty well, but gradually after my meals, in attempting to swallow a mouthful of food, part would come through my nostrils, and part go into my wind-pipe, and I would be choked.

Q. That is just the bother? A. Yes, sir.

Q. [To the Students.] This man has partial paralysis of the superior muscle of the pharynx, and besides that inflammation of the perichondrium.

Q. Are you growing worse? A. Yes; gradually growing worse.

Q. How old are you? A. Fifty-five.

Q. And you have enjoyed tolerably good health? A. Yes, sir.

Q. Did you, in your younger days, bolt your food; do you now eat in a hurry? A. Most generally, like men in business.

Q. Very hot and cold things make no difference to you? A. No, sir. I swallow them all alike.

Q. And then you run off to work with your mouth full? A. Yes, sir.

(To the students.) This is a trouble which may result, sooner or later, in a stricture. He has partial paralysis of the superior muscle of the pharynx, which don't act, or at least does so only partially. He takes a drink, or a sup of fluid, and he gets half through swallowing, and the action stops. You have all noticed how the œsophagus contracts in the horse when drinking water, and so it does here. These different fibres of the muscles act consecutively one after the other, and being under control of the will, all goes well, but if one set of fibres does not act in unison with the others, we have a reverse action, and part of the food is ejected, and only part goes the right way. I should suppose electricity would be a good thing to be applied here to the neck, and I would also administer cocculus. I forgot you have been prescribed for; therefore you will go on and take the medicines ordered.

(The patient.) I am through with that prescription to-day.

Q. How far do you live from here? A. 20 miles.

Q. When will you see Prof. Houghton again? A. To-day.

Q. Then I will see him about it, and hope hereafter you will not only be of service to us, but that we will be some benefit to you.

Subacute Thecitis.

JAMES BROWN, *Aged Fifty-two Years.*

Prof. Helmuth.—Tell me about your disease from the beginning. A. It occurred about three years ago.

Q. This wrist became affected in the winter time? A. Yes, sir, in October.

Q. Then you had some trouble about your hip? A. Yes, sir.

Q. What kind of trouble was it in your hip? A. A severe pain.

Q. Had you sprained your hip, or had you rheumatism in your hand? A. I never did.

Q. Have you had any falls on your hip, or have you hurt it? A. No, sir.

Q. Then, afterwards, did you take medicine to relieve the pain in your joint. A. Yes; and a great deal of medicine.

Q. You plastered your hip—and everything else? A. Yes, sir.

Q. You don't know whether you were salivated? A. No, sir.

Q. How long did you have the pain of which you speak? A. Three or four weeks.

Q. Then, after that disappeared, this trouble began? A. Yes, sir.

Q. Now tell us about this. What is the trouble now; does it pain all the time? A. There is no pain at all.

Q. Is there weakness? A. Yes, sir.

Q. You have no power to move the hand? A. No; I cannot work with it.

Q. Have you ever slept this way, with your hand under your head? A. No, sir.

Q. It is not a habit of yours? A. No, sir.

(There is a disease occasioned by lying with the hand under the head, called *wrist drop*.)

Q. You have no pain at all? A. No, sir.

Q. And that don't hurt you (making pressure)? A. No, sir.

Q. You have been among physicians? A. Yes, sir.

Q. And have taken a great deal of medicine? A. Yes, sir.

Q. Can you shut your hand? (The patient endeavors to squeeze Prof. Helmuth's hand.)

Q. Is that the tightest you can shut it? A. Yes, sir; and that makes me shake all over.

He has subacute synovitis and thecitis; not only a subacute inflammation of the membranes, but of the external and internal lateral ligaments of the joint, extending into the thecæ. This is merely subacute inflammation, unaccompanied with pain—the same character of inflammation that might ultimately result in the formation of a cold abscess.

Q. What have you applied to it? A. Ice.

Q. Croton oil? A. Yes, sir.

Q. Wet bandages? A. Yes, sir.

Q. And it don't get any better? A. No, sir.

Q. Have you ever taken any homœopathic medicine for it? A. No, sir.

Q. Have you had a dry bandage over it? A. Yes, sir.

He has had the wet bandage applied to his arm, according to directions, and a dry bandage over it, which is very good. Now I will put him on a high potency of rhus, and give him two powders a day, night and morning. (To the patient.) You must take this medicine, and do nothing else. I don't want you to mix it with any other prescription. If you are under two kinds of treatment neither one will do you any good.

Surgical Clinic of February 6th, 1875.

Dr. J. H. Thompson.—This case of encysted tumor, which you saw two weeks ago, has had nothing done for it except the application of strips of adhesive plaster. The sides of the cyst have now adhered, as I then told you that they probably would. The action which nature has set up here for the cure of this case has disintegrated the cyst so that it was not necessary to remove it. Nature has performed the entire cure, just as it would if the sac had been removed before it ruptured.

Fracture of the Inferior Maxilla.

MR. PARKER, *Aged Thirty-six Years.*

Prof. Helmuth.—This patient voluntarily comes before you. He is a patient whom I attended for Dr. Belcher. As I have just lectured on fractures, I bring him before you in order that you may hear the history of the case and see the method of treatment.

The patient states that his jaw was fractured a month ago. He was at work in an ice house, and while standing at the bottom of an inclined plane, down which the ice passed with great velocity, a block of it flew off the side, at a tangent, and struck him on the face.

The jaw bone broke just at the angle. He was rendered insensible for twenty-three hours, and does not recollect anything about it. This large block of ice, coming with such velocity down the inclined plane, must have struck him with tremendous force. For a long time after I first saw him he could not get up from the bed, because of giddiness, and a certain amount of confusion of the brain—all showing that he had received a very severe concussion. Now his health is very much better, and the bone is uniting finely. I will show you the method I use for bandaging fractures like this. I first take a square piece of tin, cut the corners off, and then divide it in the middle like this (cutting the tin with pliers).

It is better to trim it out on the edge that is applied next to the neck. Then bend over the top and bottom to make it fit the chin, in this shape (bending the tin into a box shape).

Then I have a piece of buckskin sewed over the metal. The advantage of using tin is that you can measure and cut until you can make it fit any sized chin. When it is on, you can hold it very tightly indeed; and when Barton's bandage is applied over it, you have the parts very securely held. That is just as good a splint as you can make. I have treated a great many fractures with such a splint, and with good results. Two of the patient's teeth were knocked out by the blow, one of them came out and I replaced the other. When you are called to treat these injuries of the jaw, the first thing to be done is to look for loose teeth, and if you find any, remove them ; but if there is any tendency for them to be retained in their sockets, it is well to replace them and hold them in position. I have saved this man a tooth by replacing it. The patient states that he now suffers chiefly from pain through the ear. That is a symptom of disease about the jaw. He now has the incipient symptoms of what may be called "spurious anchylosis," which is very easily overcome by the necessary movement.

Injury to the Cauda Equina.

CHARLES JOSEPH VANDER, *Aged Ten Years.*

(*Mrs. Vander* states the history of the case.) This boy, when four years old, was taken with pain, and would complain of it on every attempt to move or play. A physician treated him for rheumatism and then for white swelling, and then he applied a splint. He continued to get steadily worse. He was then sent to Dr. Taylor, who immediately pronounced it the hip complaint, and said that a splint must be applied. He was under his care for six months. No abscess or swelling had then appeared. When the pain was very great the doctor directed the extension of the splint by means of the key. The doctor kept the splint on for four years—always promising to cure him. He would give an opiate when there was an increase of pain, but in spite of the opium he suffered greatly. It required from three to five drops of the liquid opium, once, twice, and sometimes five times in a night to get him to sleep. The doctor made plenty of promises He kept the splint on for three years, then took it off, and pronounced the boy cured, and directed that he be taken home and turned out and fed.

Prof. Helmuth.—That is the way they use old horses when they turn them out to die.

Mrs. Vander.—He still suffered a great deal of pain at times. By this time the pain had extended to both legs. It seemed like rheumatic pain. The boy was then taken to Dr. Schaeffer, and he also promised to cure him if put under his care, and said that *he would have cured him before* if the patient had been brought to him, and that it was a great pity that he had not seen him before. Dr. Schaeffer tried all the skill that he was possessed of, and continued adjusting the splint and giving medicine, and always *promising.*

Prof. Helmuth.—I shall be very careful how I promise anything.

Mrs. Vander.—This continued until February, a year ago. Then Dr. Schaeffer told me that he could not fail after awhile to bet otally cured, but wanted me to get Dr. John Wood to tell him what was the matter; but as Dr. Wood was in New York, and I live in Brooklyn, I preferred to go to a physician in Brooklyn. Dr. Schaeffer wanted to hold on to *one* leg with a splint, while I got Dr. Hutchins to attend to the *other* leg; but I was not willing he should; and so I had Dr. Hutchins to attend him for six months. He relieved him somewhat of the pain. He said the child was suffering from contraction of the muscles. Although he relieved him somewhat of pain, the lack of muscular power was just as bad. Dr. Hutchins then said that he had done all that he could, after treating him six months, and said that he would never be any better. Then I called in Dr. Lord. He used electricity for six months, and the consequence was that the muscles of the leg relaxed, and the pain became much easier. Before that the legs were held tightly together at the knee. He has had more motion since than he had before the application of electricity. Dr. Lord gave him medicine at the same time, and I think that he was benefited quite a good deal by the treatment. There is still a great weakness in his spine. He can use his limbs, or turn, or roll around, but he cannot raise his body up without great pain.

Prof. Helmuth.—This is one of those cases that need to be studied from beginning to end. The disease has been obscure from the very first day of its appearance; and when we see it now, in its better developed form, we have no right to cast a shadow of reproach upon those other physicians who have seen it in its obscure state, because we do not know when we may ourselves have to pronounce upon just such a condition. There are certain obscure diseases in surgery, whether in the formation of abscesses, imperfectly developed hip disease, or irritation of the spine, which are very difficult to diagnose until they are fully developed. It is not, therefore, our province to throw discredit on any one, because in the earlier stages of the disease the diagnosis was not made out as we now see that it ought to have been. Let us always keep this before us in surgery. Rather than now blame any treatment that has been applied, we will take it for granted that these gentlemen all did what they thought was best. No matter what school a man may belong to, we cannot believe that he is dishonest when he takes charge of a case of this kind, or that he does not do his best. It is the lack of proper attention which constitutes malpractice. We take it for granted that the majority of respectable physicians, when they have a case of this character, do their very best. It is unfortunate when they do not succeed; but it is not for us to sit in judgment upon what they do. Doctors, as a general rule, are honest, true hearted men, no matter to what school they may belong; and if ministers of the gospel would pay half as much attention to the members of their flocks as the generality of doctors do to their patients, then, in the day of judgment, the devil will be most egregiously disappointed.

In examining this patient I shall first look to see if his prepuce is elongated. Sometimes the removal of the prepuce has great effect in alleviating these symptoms. There are cases on record where simulated hip diseases have been relieved by the excision of the fore skin, strange as that may appear. You see that the prepuce of this patient is very much elongated. An adhesion has been formed on the side.

Q. Did this child, when he was four years old, have any fall?

Mrs. Vander.—Yes; he fell out of his wagon. In going over a curbstone the wagon tilted and he fell out. I do not know where he struck. That was between the ages of three and four years. He appeared to be well afterwards. I do not know that he sustained any injury at the time, but it was during that year that he first began to show symptoms of disease.

Prof. Helmuth.—My own little boy fell out of a wagon in the same way when he was three years old, and he was paralyzed for two years afterwards. The splints are off now ; he is twelve years old, and he is getting well.

You can trace this disease straight back to that injury. This child has no hip disease ; but he has disease of the cauda equina, or nerves which go down on each side of the spinal marrow, and which cause contraction of the adductor muscles of the thigh. All of these muscles are very stiff. The use of electricity has done him a great deal of good—perhaps more good than anything else. I do not promise anything about this patient. I will have a consultation with Prof. Burdick about it. I do not think that the child has anything the matter with either hip. I think that the trouble is in the spine, resulting from the injury that the nerves received when he fell. We move our bodies by the muscles that are supplied by the nerves that come from the spine ; and if you injure a part of those nerves, a species of paralysis of certain muscles usually follows. This boy has a variety of paralysis of the rotator muscles. These cases in their incipient stages are very difficult to diagnose—much more difficult than in an advanced stage like the present. Recollect what I told you about the elongation of the prepuce. The first thing, probably, that I shall do in this case will be to circumcise the patient.

Fracture of Lower Third of the Ulna.

JULIA MURRAY, *Aged Forty Years.*

History of Case.—(On Sunday last, at about half past 11, as I was coming out of the Grand Hotel, I slipped and fell. My feet slipped out from under me, and I put my hard behind me and fell directly on the wrist. I went back to my hotel, and a gentleman stretched out my arm, and then told me to go to a doctor. I went to a physician on 31st street and Broadway. The doctor said that the bone was broken, and he set it. It gave me a great deal of pain.)

Prof. Helmuth.—This is a fracture of the lower end of the ulna.

It does not extend down into the joint, but the bone is cracked obliquely. (Removes the bandage and splints.) You notice that the Doctor had put on the lower portion of this splint a compress, in order to raise the lower fragment. This was very well, but it has pressed it up most too high, and it has produced excoriation on the under surface. We shall apply on this a little tenax, put on a patent felt splint, and then the patient will be more comfortable. In putting on the bandage we must be careful not to apply it so tightly as to arrest the circulation; but it must be employed so as to prevent the friction of the splint, and because she has quite severe excoriations both above and below. We will use tenax on each side, and then put on a bandage before applying the splint. You must not understand this bandage to be the same kind that is used next to the skin before we apply a splint. It is merely a substitute for a lining to the splint, and that is all; as a rule, a bandage next to the skin, unless it be for the purpose of preventing excoriation, ought not to be used, for it sometimes causes a great deal of trouble and swelling. (The Professor asks a student to apply the bandage.) A little practice is worth all the talk in the world. It is easy to criticise a magnificent picture, and to say that this part and that are bad, but it is a very difficult thing to do the work yourself. It is very easy to criticise the work of others, and very often people criticise things that they could not begin to do themselves. The worst critics are generally the biggest asses.

Now that the bandage is on we will put on Ahll's patent felt splint, and secure it with adhesive straps.

Aneurism of the Aorta.

I now have a case which it gives me a great deal of pleasure to be able to show you. I am apt to be a little careful in my statements of what can, and what cannot be done by internal medication. I am rather disposed to be skeptical than otherwise, as you all know; but when I say that I have a case here, that I believe is almost cured, of aneurism of the arch of the aorta, I believe that I am stating very nearly the fact. At all events I now have a patient to show you, who presented all the symptoms of aneurism of the arch of the aorta on the right side; and who was certainly sent home to die. The most peculiar train of symptoms were developed in his case, I think, that I have ever known; yet here he is—able to go out; and with a beating of his heart that is almost natural. Mr. Porter was a resident of China. From what he tells me I infer that there are a great many cases of this form of disease in that locality. I do not know why it should be so, but so it is. He was first taken with intermittent fever at a town on the Yang-Tse-Kiang River, and had it for nearly a month. After that, he suffered a great deal of pain all through his chest. Then the doctor ordered a change of climate. (That is always a bad sign—when a doctor orders a change of climate you may be sure that there is something the matter with the patient.) His trouble was called "Rheumatism of the heart." He then went to Shanghai and was attended by a French physician; he stayed there a month and improved, but then the trouble began to develop again. He had great pulsation from the slightest cause, and all the time; he had also a great deal of neuralgia in the side of his head, and particularly on the left side. Motion became almost impossible, on account of the violence of the pulsation, which any attempt to move was sure to produce. He then went four hundred miles further south, but the trouble still continued. There he was treated by an English physician, who called the disease aneurism of the heart, but did not like to tell the patient any particulars. He was so weak that the doctor thought he would die before he could get to Japan. Then he went to San Francisco, and visited the Springs; and nearly died while there. The doctor there gave him some medicine which relieved him; for a time he thought that he was getting better, and then returned. He arrived there in June and had to leave in September. Then he came straight through to New York. He was brought to me by Dr. White, of Harlem; and went into the hospital on the 15th of last October. When I saw him he had no radial pulse; he had an enlargement on the upper side of the chest, and with a pulsation or bruit, which was very well marked, and of tremendous power. He was sleepless and restless, and suffered a great deal from neuralgia; but never lost his appetite. His digestion has been good from the first. He felt so miserable that he did not care whether he lived or died. His heart is now beating rather louder than usual; which I account for by the fact that he has not been about long, and coming to see you and telling his case has given him a little nervous palpitation. The bruit is now entirely gone. When he is resting in bed he is very comfortable. His neuralgia has all disappeared. His heart is beating about three times as loud as it generally does, because he is a little excited.

I gave this patient ½ drachm of gallic acid three times per day—that is about 90 grains per day; and five drops of sub-sulphate of iron three times per day on alternate days. Gallic acid has a specific action on the blood, and has a tendency to coagulate it. It is one of the surest medicines that can be given to arrest internal hemorrhage. I gave him this because I knew of nothing else; and because I had seen two reported cases of aneurism which were said to have been cured by its use. Two months before I had been consulted by a gentleman from Atlanta, Ga., who bore with him letters of several of the most distinguished gentlemen of New York, stating that he had aneurism of the aorta; and who had taken iodide of potash in large quantities. I ordered him the same treatment I have stated, and have received favorable reports from him. This patient had been under treatment at Atlanta, Ga., about a month, when I received this letter concerning him:

ATLANTA, GA., *Nov*, 30, '74.

WILLIAM TOD HELMUTH, M. D.

My Dear Doctor—Dr. Cleveland requests me to write you, giving a statement of Mr. F. F. Coulter's case. He was kept on gallic acid and per sulph. ferri solution, as you advised, until the first of this month, when, upon careful examination, the heart's action was found to be perfectly normal. The sufflement spoken of in our first has entirely disappeared. Pulse 72 per minute. The sound of the pulsation of the heart perfectly clear. There yet remained that huskiness of voice and some torpidity of the liver. The sclerotica slightly tinged yellow. Discontinued gallic acid and per sulph. ferri sol., and put him on digitalis $\frac{1}{10}$ dilution, 10 drops three times a day for one week. Improvement set in again after second day's use. Sclerotica clear; skin looking better; tongue cleaned off nicely; healthy in appearance; hoarseness somewhat better; continued second week digitalis.

I think from his present condition he will make a perfect recovery.

Respectfully,

F. F. FABER, M. D.

Having this case in my mind as this patient presented, I determined to give this medicine another trial, and so far it has been successful. The perturbations of the nervous system which Mr. Porter endured, when under treatment with gallic acid were very remarkable. For instance, he would lose all control of certain muscles or nerves. He would have a piece of beef on his fork, and try to put it to his mouth, but suddenly would lose control of his arm, and the meat would go over his head. He did not appear to have any control over the nerves or the voluntary muscles. Before taking the acid his hands were constantly numb.

I do not offer this treatment to you as homœopathic. I do not know exactly where to put it—whether to call it chemical, mechanical, or what not. I do not offer the remedies as infallible, nor do I know that, from the use of such large doses, harm does not result to the constitution; but if in diseases like aneurism of the aorta, which is generally and uniformly fatal, and is so acknowledged, such amelioration as I have shown you can be secured by giving these doses; then, until we know of a better plan, it is our bounden duty to administer them. If we can employ another plan, then it will be better to adopt that which is safest.

This gentleman comes to you of his own accord, at my suggestion, that I may illustrate the action of these two medicines in cases of aneurism of the aorta. I hope and believe, that with proper care and attention, he will ultimately recover entirely. Whether the pulse will ever return to its regular rate I cannot say, but he has none now. At the same time his circulation is sufficient to keep him in fair health. His spirits have been remarkably good. He has got along as well as any patient could possibly expect. But it you could have seen him when he first came to the hospital, when there was such rapid and tremendous pulsation, and he was suffering from neuralgia and sleeplessness, you would have thought the case a hopeless one. Now, I can scarcely believe him to be the same man. From the 3d to the 10th of November he expectorated a great deal of blood. This is one of the symptoms of aneurism about the larger vessels, particularly the aorta. For a number of days after he was put under treatment he spit this blood, accompanied with a great deal of phlegm, which nauseated him. That has all passed away, and he has been out riding in the park, and seems to take an interest in human life, and thinks that the best thing that he can now do—is to study medicine.

Pott's Disease.

ANTHONY ROUL, *Aged Four Years.*

We have here another case of spine disease. It seems to me that in large cities, spine diseases and affections of the joints—especially among the poorer classes—are rapidly on the increase. I have had in my office this morning three cases of spine disease, and here is another. Whether it is the method in which people live, or whether it is the inability of certain classes to obtain the necessaries of life, or whether, in the rearing of children, people are more careless than they used to be, I am unable to say; but certain it is that, in this city, spinal diseases and joint diseases are rapidly on the increase. In the country you do not meet with them. This is a case of Pott's disease of the spine, in its incipiency. This child had scarlet fever. The mother lost three from scarlet fever within a week, and this is the only one left. This disease made its appearance after the fever. The first thing to be done is to have a proper apparatus put on the child.

Paronychia Whitlow.

STEPHEN O'HARA, *Aged Fifty-four Years.*

(A felon on the third finger of the left hand, which the doctor opened).

I will apply to this felon a solution of fluoric acid—one part to 25—and one drachm of the solution to be mixed in a pint of water, and then apply it. The prescription is thus written:

℞—Fluoric Acid gtt ij.
Aquæ ℥ j.
M.

Prof. Burdick.—You must be exceedingly careful to give your patients full directions about the use of prescriptions. I once gave this prescription to a patient with directions to apply it to the finger; and he did so, without diluting it with water, and the consequence was he had a lively time.

Prof. Helmuth.—There is a history connected with prescriptions, which of course you know; and you know moreover that the first mark of the prescription—"℞"—is considered scientific, being a sign of the ancient astrologers or soothsayers. To show you how scientific some things *may look*, which are not scientific at all, I will write you a prescription—which you can take every two hours.

℞ Spiritus Vini. Gall. fl. ℥ ij.
Tinc. Gentian comp. fl. ʒ j.
Sacch. alb. pulv. coch. min. j.
Aquæ frigidæ fl. ℥ iij.
Misce bene, et adde corticis limoni seotionem parvulam.
S Ter. die hauriendum.

Congenital Hernia.

PETER WEDIN, *Aged Eight Years.*

History of Case.—(Hernia commenced when he was only a month old. A truss was worn for about twelve months, but it gave so much pain that it was then discontinued. The intestine remained within the abdomen for a while after the truss was taken off. Every time he would cry the protrusion would return.)

Prof. Helmuth.—This child has congenital enlargement of the inguinal canal. I think that he can be cured without very much trouble; but he will have to wear a truss for some time. It must not be one with too hard a pad, nor one that will cause him any irritation. The abdominal rings in children of this age will generally close up. If this child could be kept on his back and take some such medicine as nux vomica it would hasten the cure. I recommend the elastic truss, made by Rainbow, which is supported from the shoulder. Give him nux vomica three times per day.

Surgical Clinic of February 13th, 1875.

Paronychia Whitlow.

(*Continued from page* 157.)

STEPHEN O'HARA, *Aged Fifty-four Years*,

on whose finger a felon was opened one week ago, returns.

Prof. Helmuth.—In this case we applied fluoric acid in solution (see page 157), and it has done a great deal of good. He has not had any trouble with the bone, but there was a considerable discharge. I only bring him now before you in order that you may see the condition of the hand. You will find in the treatment of felons that you can always afford a great deal of relief, when they begin to suppurate, by removing all of the dead skin, which, becoming thickened, from its unyielding character, gives a great deal of pain. By taking the scissors and removing this you will relieve the patient from much suffering. Sometimes, in the earlier stages, you can make these felons abort, by dipping the finger in ley, and sometimes by placing around the finger the thin white skin which is between the shell and the white of an egg. The application of nitric acid is said, also, to sometimes make a felon abort; but when it has progressed so far that the inflammation cannot be arrested, then it is better to accelerate the suppurating process. But in the earlier stages we can, no doubt, prevent the formation of pus. It is not necessary to wait until suppuration is complete before opening the felon. In this case the process was only beginning; there was but a slight indication of the formation of pus; but I endeavored to get the knife down to the side of the bone, and the operation has been a success.

Fracture of Lower Third of the Ulna.

JULIA MURRAY, *Aged Forty Years*,

(*Continued from page* 152.)

who was before the class at the last clinic with fracture of the ulna, returns to have the arm redressed.

Prof. Helmuth.—The bone is healing as well as it can. I can feel that there is a deposit of the *provisional callous*, but I see that there is a tendency of the hand to turn inward—to turn to the radial side—and therefore we will put on a pistol shaped splint, in order to keep it in the right position. In the dressing of fractures it is astonishing how a little pressure in the right direction will prevent what would otherwise result in deformity. If, when you remove a splint to examine a fracture, you see that the bone is not straight, or that the hand is not in exactly the right position, then is the time, by the application of a pad in the right place, and by a suitably shaped splint, to prevent further deformity.

Prof. Helmuth.—Whenever a fracture takes place near the joint the inflammation extends into the sheathes of the tendons and renders them very stiff, and for that reason passive motion is always required.

(*Dr. Thompson applies the bandage.*)

Fractures of the arm unite sooner than those of the leg; the arm unites with tolerable firmness in six weeks; the thigh and leg in eight weeks.

The union of broken bones is much slower than that of the soft parts. The ends of the bone being kept steadily together they soon become surrounded by a deposit of plasma, which is gradually converted into an osseous substance, making thus a bony hoop to act as a splint to support the fragments exactly in their place. This is called provisional callous, because it only has a temporary use.

Mode of Repair.—The method which nature observes in repairing lesions of the osseous structure is most beautiful, and, when carefully noted, may be divided into several stages.

The first stage is a period of rest or incubation. The inflammatory lymph is thrown out around the site of injury, which may occupy two or three days. The tissues during this stage are soft and somewhat succulent, and infiltrated with a fluid resembling serum. This is the period of true rest, so far as the ends of the bones are concerned, which remain in a quiet condition, while nature removes the *debris*, clears away extravasated blood, takes away the swelling, and prepares for the second period.

The second stage is the period of uniting the fragments together. This is accomplished by the deposition of a fibro-gelatinous substance, of a slightly reddish tinge, which surrounds the extremities, as it were, with a pad, holding them together. This substance may also be poured out, though in a lesser degree, in the medullary canal, thus giving support both externally and internally to the fractured ends of the bone. This substance gradually, and in different ways, is transformed into the so called provisional or intermediate callus.

This substance is not bone; but in the deposit around the fracture, points of bone begin to be deposited, the fibrine poured out, becoming first cartilage, and then receiving into itself phosphate of lime, it becomes bone. A similar work is going on within, in the part called the medullary canal.

Then begins the third stage, which goes to the end of the sixth or eighth week. During this period the external and the internal deposits become completely ossified and firm, though the ends of the bone are not yet grown together.

The fourth stage extends to the end of the fifth and sixth month. During this time the external or provisional callus becomes covered with a periosteum, and the ends of the bones themselves are fastened together by a bony deposit.

The fifth stage extends from the fifth or sixth, to the twelfth month. During this time the ends of the bone become grown together so strongly that the bony ring or provisional callus is no longer wanted, and it becomes absorbed and disappears—in other words, having no further use for it, nature takes off her splint. The point of fracture is now as strong as any other part.

Union in Compound Fracture.

The union of compound fractures takes place in a different manner from that of the simple fracture just described. In this case there is suppuration, and the bones remain disunited several weeks, and there is no provisional callus formed. But after some time the ends of the bones soften and granulate; and when the production of pus declines, the granulations are gradually changed into bone.

Prof. Helmuth.—To a student of the class:

Q. Can you describe fracture of the lower jaw? A. It generally takes place near the chin. It may occur also near the angles of the jaw. It may be simple or compound, and is known by the pain, the swelling, the inability to move the jaw, the indentation felt by the finger, the irregularity of the teeth, and the grating sensation felt while moving the jaw with the hand placed on the back fragment.

Q. In a fracture of the lower jaw, what is the best bandage to be applied? A. The figure 8 bandage.

Q. Who introduced the figure bandage? A. John Rhea Barton one of the most promising surgeons that the United States ever knew; and who made himself immortal by the operation for anchylosis of the knee joint, which bears his name.

Q. When suppuration is progressing, does the patient sweat? A. When suppuration is going on in the body, particularly if there is any amount of pus forming, there is profuse sweating. This is one of the symptoms of the disease. Not only is this sweat profuse, but the character of the coldness and shivering is peculiar, and appears at regular intervals. Many a case of suppuration in malarious localities has been mistaken for intermittent fever. A chill comes on in the afternoon, followed by fever and profuse sweat; and these are the symptoms which may lead you astray when suppuration is about to commence. It is by means of these symptoms that we diagnose the formation of cold abscesses in obscure places.

Inflamed Ulcer.

SOPHIA BARTLETT, *Aged Forty-one Years.*

History of the Case.—"I have had this sore on my leg for about a month. At first there came an inflammation extending about three or four inches. Then three or four purple marks came around it, and it spread rapidly. It broke the next day. When it first made its appearance, I put sweet oil on it, because I thought it was only a little pimple. Then I put on spermaceti ointment, to cure it. Then I was told to use Dally's salve. The inflammation still kept spreading."

Prof. Helmuth.—Here is a case of irritable ulcer, or, what should more properly be called in the wider classification, "an inflamed sore." You will recollect that this variety is different from the irritable, because the inflammatory action seems to extend to a greater degree around the former. When we have an inflamed sore we not only have the ulceration which is extending at the localized point, but we generally have a diffuse inflammatory action throughout the connective tissue Ultimately, this high degree of inflammatory action will disappear and the patient will seem to be better constitutionally; but we will have a change taking place in the surface of the ulcer itself; and then will present the old fashioned variety of ulcer, with no disposition to heal, and with scarcely any granulation visible. These are the sores that we frequently see in persons of her position in life, who are unable to lay aside work. If she could go home and secure the right kind of treatment—which we will prescribe—keeping her leg in an elevated position for three or four weeks—that ulcer could be cured without the slightest difficulty. But if we have to strap it, and support the parts with a bandage, so that she can perform the ordinary avocations of life, it will be a very different thing to manage, and the cure will be tedious. The patient says that her foot hurts her more when it is elevated than when it is down. Why is this? Because the parts are in a congested condition; but if she will persist in keeping the foot elevated, and let sufficient blood out of the distended capillaries, then the reverse will be true; and she will have less pain when the foot is elevated than when it is dependent; for when it hangs the blood will rush into it and it will begin to throb, and beat, and burn. In such a condition as this, the first thing to be done is to allay the local irritation. The diffuse inflammatory action is extending along the connective tissue and renders any pressure upon the foot almost unbearable. The best thing to reduce this inflammation is a simple cold water application.

She must keep the leg elevated; then take a piece of canton flannel, or old muslin, and fold it four times upon itself; dip this compress in cold water, wring it sufficiently to prevent its dripping, and envelop the leg therewith; over that, wrap a piece of dry canton flannel, and over that, a piece of oiled silk, and tie it on with three or four tapes. I venture to say, that she will not have the wet bandage on that sore but a few minutes before the rag will be so dry that it will have to be rewetted. She will have to keep rewetting it as often as it becomes dry. As the inflammatory action disappears, it will take longer for the bandage to dry. For the first day or two it will have to be wet two or three times in an hour. She must keep her leg on a chair, and the water by her side, and as often as the bandage becomes dry, remove it, wet, and apply it over and over again. Internally, she had better have aconite. After the inflammation has subsided we will then come to the treatment of the ulcer. What shall we do with that? Put mud or dry earth on it. The wet earth treatment is almost as good as the dry. If you apply earth after the inflammatory action has subsided you will find that in less than four days you will have a granulating surface where there is none now. During the first three days the fœtor and the discharge will increase, then a slough will separate from the centre of the sore, and you will have a granulating surface appearing. You can continue applying the earth, and if you desire to hasten the cure you can strap it every day, and give internally silicea, calcarea, mercurius, or any of the medicines which the constitution seems to indicate. But in the first stages you must give medicines to subdue the constitutional disturbance and keep the blood out of the capillaries; then give something to stimulate the ulcer, and, finally, promote the process of granulation and cicatrization.

Traumatic Gangrene.

I expected that I would have an amputation to perform this morning, but the case would not keep. It was a bad case of traumatic gangrene—worse than I had any idea of—and as soon as I saw it, though it was at night, I was obliged to remove the arm. As I told you, when speaking of traumatic gangrene, you are never to wait for the line of demarcation. The accident in this case occurred on Monday night. On Tuesday I received a telegram, asking if I could come over and see it. I telegraphed back to bring the patient to the hospital. He was caught between two cars, he does not know exactly how, and the arm was terribly mangled I did not see the case until Thursday at half past four in the afternoon, and then the gangrene was rapidly extending. In three hours it had increased two inches; and, at half past seven in the evening I could barely find flap enough to make Larrey's amputation at the shoulder joint; however, I succeeded in so doing. When I took hold of the tissues I could feel them crepitate in my fingers. The veins across the shoulders were very much enlarged, showing that the grangene was invading those parts. I do not now know what will be the result of the case. When I heard of it I thought it was one which would keep for a few days, and that I could bring it before the class; but it was ordained otherwise. The man would not have lived through the night.

Hip Joint Disease.

AUGUST SISSMAN, *Aged Twelve Years.*

(*Continued from pages* 60, 105, 116 and 142)

Here is our friend August Sissman. I told him to come at the last clinic, and here he is. He is very much improved in every way. (Holding up the splint which the boy had taken off.)

The counter extension in these splints is made by means of the perineal band, which passes up into the perinæum and fastens to the crutch at the top. The extension in this case is made from the shoe. In Dr. Taylor's splint the extension is kept up continually, and there is a bar that goes across under the foot. In Dr. Sayres' splint there is no shoe, but the extension is maintained by bands of adhesive plaster, which have a tendency to draw the leg down. Recollect that the Bauers' splint has the shoe; Taylor's, the bar of iron under the shoe; Sayres', held in situ by adhesive plasters.

You see that these sores have nearly healed, and, if it were not for the friction of this splint, the larger one would be closed entirely. The openings behind are not yet quite cured. You will recollect what an aggravated case this was. You see that his leg has come down about two inches and a half. This was a case in the third stage of hip disease; the improvement so far has been quite remarkable. There is some diseased bone there yet, which may ultimately necessitate an excision of the head of the femur. During the time he has been under treatment the leg has lengthened; his appetite is good, he sleeps well at night, he has less pallor, and no hectic flush. Taking all of these symptoms into consideration, we can say that there has been a general improvement in his case, which is indicated by these favorable constitutional symptoms. We can say, that the hopes of recovery are good, when we see that the constitutional tendency of the patient is to improve.

If he was run down like the man Hart, whom you saw, there would be but little hope. Hart, you will remember, had two or three openings into the scrotum. In such a case an operation would have been entirely out of the question. He died in a most miserable condition, worn out by the constitutional irritation and the profuseness of the discharge. At the time he was here he had twenty-eight openings. The discharge was so great that when he would raise up he would leave about two quarts of pus in the paper which was used as a dressing.

This patient is a great deal better in every way. He has had nothing internally but calcarea and silicea.

Prof. Burdick, of the obstetrical department, proposes next week to honor us with the presentation of his prizes, which will assist to leave pleasant memories not only of these clinics, but of all who have taken part in them. I hope that when you come to the practical part of your profession—particularly in the obstetrical department—you will be able to know a head presentation from a wind bag!

Our clinics this session have been remarkably well attended and supplied with patients. They have been attended not only by the gentlemen of the class, but by outside physicians, and by members of the faculty, who have been regularly present. I regard this, not only as complimentary to you, but also as a compliment to myself. We were carried a little out of our usual line in clinics, by the case of subclavian aneurism, and, because of our attention to that subject, we were not able to lecture much on amputations. I believe that when we have finished with the latter we will have gotten through a pretty complete surgical course.

When we take into consideration the number of patients we have had at these clinics, I think we may congratulate ourselves, that the facilities in the surgical department of the Homœopathic College have been equal to those of any institution extant. I do not say this as a boast; I only mean to say that I am supplied with facilities for teaching, and it affords you opportunities for seeing, the practical results of medicines administered according to the homœopathic law.

I long ago made it a rule never to perform operations before the class which all could not see, because those operations are not only uninteresting to lookers on, but they become very tedious. Therefore, while I have lectured upon, and shown you cases of cleft palate, fistulæ, and diseases of the nose, I have performed the operations at the hospital and brought the patients here to you afterwards that you might see the results. I trust, therefore, gentlemen, that though you have all had a great deal to do this winter, that you have had some pleasant times at these clinics. Next Monday week is the birthday of Washington, and is properly regarded as a national holiday; I shall, however, continue my lectures on amputations, and, although I do not make the attendance at all compulsory, I would like to see as many of you as possible here, because I have been unavoidably detained from lecturing on that subject, having so much to teach on aneurism. After I had lectured to you on the case of cleft palate I took the patient to the hospital and operated. Probably only two or three could have seen it had I closed the cleft here. I always endeavor to bring before the class all the operations which can be seen; but those which are tedious I prefer to do elsewhere, and bring the report of the case, with the patient, or *perhaps the specimen*, before the class, so that you may know the result.

Of all the lectures that I deliver I regard the clinics as the most agreeable. I like them, because I endeavor to make them a little free and easy for you, and because I can vary a little in the subject. If there is anything that I do dislike, it is to occupy an entire hour talking on one dry subject, without variation. Many a time I have stopped and told a story, when I have seen a man nodding. Just as soon as the little narrative begins, he wakes up and is as bright as a dollar.

As this is the last clinic before examination I have to thank you very kindly for your attendance, and for the decorous manner in which you have always conducted yourselves in my presence, not only in the clinics, but everywhere else. So far as I know, not a single unpleasant circumstance has occurred between us, to mar the harmony of our friendship, which I hope will long continue to exist. If, at any time hereafter, when you have received your "sheepskins," and enter upon professional life, I can be of the slightest service to you in surgery, you can always write to me, and I will do all that in me lies for you. But do not be egotistical. Do not, if called to a case you do not understand, endeavor to treat it entirely yourself. If you do not send for me, call for some one who makes such cases a specialty. Recollect it is no disgrace to say "I do not know." It is a great deal better to say "I do not know, but I will call a consultation," than it is to be sued for $10,000 damages. Nine tenths of the suits for malpractice could be avoided, if consultations were called at the proper time. Young men have very erroneous ideas about consultations. They think that summoning a brother physician in counsel, proves derogatory to their wisdom as doctors. So they hold on to a case in the hope that it will all come right in the end. Although dame Nature does a great deal for surgery, and helps the doctor out of a great many scrapes, it is better not to urge her too far. Therefore, when you have an obscure case, do not be afraid to ask advice; and if you cannot get it where you are, you will always readily receive it from the New York Homœopathic Medical College. Whether I am here or not, you may be sure the desired assistance and information will come. But if you disregard your Alma Mater, sometime she may disown you.

Gentlemen, when you return to your homes, and look back upon this course of lectures, I trust that you may consider these clinics as among the pleasantest hours of your student days.

To Prof. S. P. BURDICK, Dr. J. H. THOMPSON, and to all who have assisted us in these surgical clinics.

GENTLEMEN—For the students and myself I tender you our *best regards, wishes, and many thanks* for the obligations we are under for the valuable services you have rendered to the class; and for the many interesting cases you have presented for our instruction. We regret that the end of the clinical term has come, but trust we shall see you at our next session of 1875–76, which promises in every respect, to prove equal, if not superior in clinical facilities, to the one which is now passed.

NEW YORK, *February* 25*th*, 1875.

To Prof. HELMUTH.

My Dear Doctor—I offer to you this Report of your Surgical Clinics as a token of my regard and respect for you, and for your ability as a Clinical Teacher. I have no expectation of pecuniary or other reward from you or the New York Homœopathic Medical College for the labor I have undertaken, save the approval of yourself and the Faculty.

Yours, very truly,

PHILETUS J. STEPHENS.

REPORT OF THE SURGICAL CLINICS HELD AT THE NEW YORK HOMŒOPATHIC COLLEGE BY WM. TOD HELMUTH, M. D., FOR THE SESSION OF 1873 AND 1874.

Acute Necrosis.

JOSEPHINE WALSH, *Aged Nine Years*,

was taken three months ago with swelling of cheek, with general febrile condition. Four teeth were extracted by a dentist, which aggravated the symptoms. She then had a very offensive breath, with profuse discharge of saliva and pus. Five weeks ago an abscess formed and discharged itself under the chin, after which the breath was not so offensive. Probe introduced, roughened and loose bone encountered.

Pronounced acute necrosis of inferior maxillary. Merc. protoiodide 30, grs. ij., night and morning for one week, and parts syringed twice a day with Lister's sol. carbolic acid.

Nov. 1, Better. Treatment continued.

Empyema.

JAMES B. CORKEY, *Aged Twenty-one Years*.

Pleuritic abscesses on left side below nipple, the lower one admitting probe one half inch; discharge freely; have existed fifteen months; œdema of both legs; mother died of phthisis.

Pronounced empyema caused by pleurisy. Sulphur 30 trit., powder every night, with injections of carbolic acid.

The differences between empyema, emphysema and hydrothorax were pointed out, and the causes of the dropsy explained. Allusion was also made to the immense amount of purulent formation which could accumulate and be discharged. The method of puncturing the thoracic walls with the aspirator, an instrument which has of late attracted great attention from the profession, was explained.

Amputation of Breast.

MRS. CUNNINGHAM, *Aged Forty-eight Years.*

Encephaloid tumor of left mamma, size of walnut, hard, purple and unbroken. Etherized, and tumor dissected out down to ribs and sternum, leaving an opening several inches in diameter.

She had been operated on by Prof. H. sixteen months ago for a similar tumor, and was then told that it would return. Previous to first operation the tumor had almost disappeared under conium mac., prescribed by Dr. Dunham, when an injury reproduced it. Wound sprayed with carbolic acid, packed with carbolized cotton, and adhesive straps applied.

Wound showed healthy granulations, and good recovery expected. It was strapped firmly to bring edges of wound together, and Fowler's solution, gtt. ij., twice a day, ordered. The only unfavorable symptoms following the operation were intermittent pulse, found to be idiopathic, and retention of urine, which was relieved by acon. and canthar. Strangury, retention of urine and intermittent pulse often follow operations, and the last may be a bad indication, and dangerous in inverse proportion to the strength of patient's constitution. In a few days more the patient left the hospital, the wound having healed very kindly.

Talipes Equino-Varus.

WM. DOHN, *Aged Four Years.*

Talipes equino-varus, operated upon one year ago, but operation rendered fruitless by the patient not wearing the proper shoe. Tendo Achillis and tibialis anticus divided subcutaneously, and shoe ordered to be worn at once.

Epithelioma of Mamma.

BRIDGET MCNALLY, *Aged Fifty-four Years.*

(*See Page* 30.)

Passed climacteric ten years ago. Two years since a small hard lump appeared in right mamma; it was painful; the nipple was retracted. The integument then ulcerated, and the peculiar granular appearance, with occasional hemorrhages, which belong to epithelioma, was noticed. The two different varieties of epithelioma, superficial and deep seated, were explained, and the arguments for and against operative measures in cancer pointed out. The value of ars., hydrast., conium, sepia, and phytolacca were noted, and the patient promised to return at the next clinic.

Sebaceous Tumor in Scalp.

MARGARET CAULDWELL, *Aged Forty-eight Years.*

Sebaceous tumor of the scalp, situated in the occiput; appeared two years ago. It gave but little inconvenience, but was growing rapidly; it had attained the size of a large walnut. Dissected out entire. The various forms of cystic tumors were mentioned.

Internal Hemorrhage and Fissure in the Anus.

MRS. R., *Aged Forty-five Years.*

This case was a very aggravated one, had existed for a number of years, was accompanied by anal spasm, and rendered the patient very miserable. Hemorrhoids removed by the platina wire brought to a white heat by the galvano-caustic battery. There was no hemorrhage. The fissures were divided throughout their extent. The cure of fissures and cracks about the anus may be sometimes accomplished by the forcible dilatation of the sphincter.

Impediment in Speech.

JOS. BROTHERFIELD, *Aged Five Years,*

Brought here supposed to be tongue tied, but it was discovered that he had nursed well, could talk fairly, and project tongue. Slight impediment in speech, due to lack of education of certain muscles. No operation required.

Spurious Anchylosis of Knee Joint.

LENA ELCESSE, *Aged Six Years*,

Two years ago fell and injured her knee, which became very much swollen. Iodine was applied, then she was put in bed, and extension by means of a two pound weight kept up. Spurious anchylosis took place nine months ago, and Professor Helmuth divided tendons of external hamstring, and ordered motion. She can now walk fairly, but there is still much swelling of the joint, with atrophy of muscle of the leg. Rhus tox. internally. Anchylosis splint ordered.

Anchylosis of Shoulder.

RACHEL MCPHERSON, *Aged Fourteen Years.*

Spurious anchylosis of right shoulder.

Humerus closely adhered to scapula, which latter had great latitude of motion; crepitus *felt* on motion; pain worse in winter. Had taken rhus tox 3, one year ago without effect. Anchylosis from chronic rheumatic arthritis. Operation recommended.

Enchondroma.

MRS. S., *Aged Forty-two Years.*

Tumor beneath middle third of clavicle; came two months ago. Pains like sticking with a needle; no pain from pressure; firmly adhered to subjacent structures. Pronounced enchondroma, and she is to return in a fortnight for removal. The peculiarities of cartilaginous growths were mentioned, their connection with bones, and those most obnoxious to their formation were alluded to.

Sebaceous Tumor of Scalp.

JOANNA SCHANAHAN, *Aged Twenty-four Years.*

Sebaceous tumor of the scalp, which was already suppurating, was left to take care of itself. Very often, either from injury or from efforts of nature to remove abnormal formation, suppuration occurs in cysts, and cures may be spontaneous. In this case such a process is going on, and a cure may probably result. Adhesion, either taking place within the walls of the sac or the cyst wall, being removed by ulceration.

Ganglion.

JOHN FORSYTHE, *Aged Nineteen Years.*

Tumor of right little finger, palmar surface hard, movable; is accustomed to lift heavy packages; noticed first appearance about a year ago, after a sprain; feeling of crepitation along flexor tendons of the wrist when exercised. Pronounced enlarged bursa of flexor tendon, with diffuse ganglion at wrist. The contents of a bursa vary; sometimes it is a straw colored fluid, sometimes of the consistence and appearance of honey; sometimes it resembles the vitreous of the eye; sometimes there are cartilaginous formations, which are discharged, which resemble the seeds of a melon; this variety of growth is called a melon seed bursa. A ganglion is an adventitious bursa. Bursæ are subject to inflammation, which may terminate in suppuration, and even gangrene. Sometimes bursæ rupture spontaneously. The methods of treatment are: sudden forcible pressure; puncture with scarification of sac internally to cause adhesions; painting with iodine externally and internally; longitudinal incision along palm of hand to relieve traction; insertion of seton through the sac. In this case a seton was passed through the sac, and cantharides applied to palm to blister.

Some improvement; crepitation partially disappeared. Cantharides collodion continued.

No improvement since last week. Palm so hard cannot be blistered by cantharides. Apply croton oil; take internally iodide of potash, and use continued pressure. This case returned in a week, being very much relieved. The treatment continued.

Node.

JOHN S., *Aged Sixty-six Years,*

About two months since injured his head by striking it forcibly against a door. Periosteal inflammation was set up; pain severe, worse at night. Now a node presents itself, which is painful on pressure, and fluctuates. On lancing, there exudes blood, and a very fetid pus, produced by caries. Pronounced periostitis and caries. Ordered wound to be packed with lint saturated with—

℞ Carbolic acid, ʒj.
Sweet Oil, ℥v.
Water, ℥iij.

Nævus.

GRACE BRINKENDAL, *Aged Eight Months.*

Capillary nævus on forehead; operated on five months ago, but has returned. Operation performed by placing suture pins through the tissues under the nævus in the form of an X, and drawing tense a ligature under these pins. If nitric acid is applied as soon as the red spots appear it will destroy the nævus, if small. Continued pressure is another means used to kill nævi. The methods by galvanic puncture, vaccination, etc., were explained.

Synovitis.

PAT WHALEN, *Aged Fifty-six Years,*

Thrown from a wagon two months since, striking his shoulder, in which joint there is dull, aching pain, worse at night. He was made to go through the motions which diagnose dislocation, and the various positions explained to the class. There were no signs of luxation, and the affection was pronounced synovitis. Rhus tox. topically and internally. Synovitis may, unless treated, proceed to spurious anchylosis; but the timely administration of medicine and passive motion will, in the majority of cases, prevent such a result. The diagnosis between spurious anchylosis and true synostosis was entered upon and explained at length.

Erosion of Inner Canthus.

MR. TURNER, *Aged Sixty-four Years.*

About five years ago inflammation began at inner canthus of left eye. Gradually the erosion has extended, now involving the lower lid. Resembles epithelioma. Diagnosis obscure. Pus must be examined for epithelial cells with microscope. A portion of the discharge was obtained for this purpose, and, in the meanwhile, prescribed hydrastis 6m.

Fistula in Ano.

HUGH KELLEY, *Aged Thirty-six Years.*

Operated on seven years ago at Brooklyn Hospital. Owing to imprudence the cut has never properly healed. The sinus was slit up and the fissures divided at the bottom. The wound was packed with prepared lint. The first appearance of fistulæ, their varieties, and methods of treatment, by knife, ligature, paralyzing the sphincter, and internal medication, were detailed to the class.

Exostosis of Great Toe.

EDMONIS WALKER, *Aged Twenty Years.*

Fungus growth and ingrowing toe nail of left great toe, which had existed for several years. On cutting into the fungus it was found to be an *osseous* growth from the phalanx, probably produced by irritation by the ingrowing nail. The whole outgrowth was excised, with the ingrown portion of the nail. Usually a very good treatment for ingrown toe nail is to shave its middle with glass, cut a notch at the apex of the nail, and raise the edges by placing underneath them small bits of lead.

Bursa.

ANTOINE LAVELLE, *Aged Thirty-three Years.*

Diffuse adventitious bursa at wrist. About three months since wrist sprained and bruised by a fall; has gradually increased in size; crepitation present. Apply pressure and blister. Introducing seton would in this case probably cause contraction of tendons.

Much better under cantharides application.

Housemaid's Knee.

MIRANDA ROY, *Aged Twenty-nine Years.*

Housemaid's knee is an enlargement of the bursa under the tendon of the extensor muscles of the thigh. It had not proceeded to ulceration. Ordered compress and cantharides, with leg as much as possible in horizontal position. May become necessary hereafter to inject iodine to excite adhesive inflammation. "Housemaid's knee," "weaver's bottom," "miner's elbow," "bunion," and the enlargement found in severe cases of talipes equino-varus, were described.

Ulceration of the Articular Cartilages.

ALBERT SWAN, *Aged Sixteen Years.*

Disease of knee joint. Ten years ago fell on the ice. Inflammation and suppuration followed, and spiculæ of bone came out. Has improved very much for the last six months under silicea, which is continued. In the first stage of this disease, when caused as above, a blood-blister is formed, and, although there is little pain, then is the time to commence treatment. If no care is exercised, inflammation proceeds to suppuration. All pressure must be taken from the joint, and the patient not allowed to walk.

Tumor on Neck.

AUGUST GRIESS, *Aged Thirty-four Years.*

Tumor of the size of an orange on left side of neck, under superficial fascia; lobulated; supposed to be cystic; fluctuation detected. Began to grow about eight months since. Operation postponed at request of patient.

Hypospadias.

A. B., *Aged Twenty-six Years.*

In hypospadias the outlet of the urethra is on the under surface of the penis, in epispadias the opening is on the upper surface; the disease is congenital. In this case the opening is in middle third of the corpus spongiosum, no normal meatus being present. There is also fissure of the glans. Penis is bent as in chordee. Urethroplasty may be performed for the cure of this affection, but in this case no operation was desired by the patient.

Preternatural Enlargement of Mammary Gland.

KATIE WARD, *Aged Twelve Years.*

Swelling of left mammary gland; not painful. Has been painted with iodine, and improved under it. Prescribed phos. 30 once a day for a week. The use of this medicine in hypertrophy of the mammæ, as well as in mammary abscess, was highly extolled.

Caries of Femur.

DENIS McDONALD, *Aged Forty-six Years.*

Fistulous opening in right thigh, lower third, from caries of femur. When a boy, injured the thigh, and spiculæ of bone came out. Two years ago last May a small tumor appeared on outside of thigh, which grew, and, in about four months, burst, and from it exuded pus, which has continued since. Probing discovers caries, but not necrosis.

Prescribed silic. [200.] Hopes to cure without use of knife. Carious bone under the probe has a *granular feel.* Above case has been at other college clinics without benefit.

Wound of Mouth.

JAMES LEET, *Aged Fifteen Months.*

Laceration of tissues of roof of mouth, from falling on a key. Some of the tissues hung by a pedicle, necessitating sloughing if left to themselves. These tissues were excised with scissors.

Spurious Anchylosis of Lower Jaw.

MARY BEAUMET, *Aged Sixteen Years.*

(*See page* 83.)

Spurious anchylosis of lower jaw, from gangrene of the mouth. Cicatrix extensive and firmly adhered to jaw. The adhesions were very fibrous, and were divided carefully within the mouth with the knife; then Westmoreland's instrument was applied and the anchylosis broken up. On the inside, between the cheek and jaw, was placed a moderately thick layer of tin foil, to prevent the adhesions recurring. Ordered to move the jaw every three hours, forcibly, to prevent the return of the anchylosis.

The diagnosis between false and true anchylosis of the jaw is this: If the patient can produce contraction of the masseter muscle the anchylosis is spurious. Anchylosis, as regards position, may be of three kinds: 1. The condyle may be fixed in the glenoid cavity. 2. The coronoid process may become attached to the zygoma. 3. The adhesion may take place between the upper and lower alveolar processes. The first is by far the most common form.

Necrosis.

GEO. PIERCE, *Sailor*, *Aged Fifty-one Years.*

Fell, about a year and a half ago, and fractured his jaw about one inch to right of symphysis. Bones were not properly adjusted, and necrosis of part of inferior maxillary has taken place. For last six months his general health has improved, and the separation of bone promoted by the use of hecla lava.

Diffuse Adventitious Bursa.

Much better, under local application of cantharides and continued pressure. Treatment continued.

Bursa.

ANTOINE LAVELLE, *Aged Thirty-three Years.*

(*Continued from page* 178.)

Much improved, less crepitation, under croton oil to blister, and internal administration of iodide of potash. Continue iodide of potash.

Crepitation at wrist has entirely disappeared, but the bursa at little finger, not yielding to previous treatment, was dissected out.

Hypospadias.

HENRY M., *Aged Six Years.*

The first step of the operation for the removal of this condition is to reëstablish the urethral opening anterior to the seat of the affection. This must be accomplished by means of a *blunt probe;*

otherwise extensive laceration may occur. The adhesions must be prevented from recurring. The second step can be performed after a few days, and consists in the occlusion of the hypospadias with sutures, and the introduction of a catheter, to carry off the urine, that it does not come in contact with the inflamed parts. This operation is not always successful.

Re-Amputation of Finger.

NANCY F., *Aged Forty-eight Years.*

Necrosis of the bone of third finger of right hand, resulting from a fall. Nine weeks ago amputation was performed, the case being treated at the College Dispensary. The disease has recurred. Amputation is now necessary, a second time. In amputations, leave sufficient flap to prevent retraction. Dr. Thompson then reamputated at the meta-carpo-phalangeal bone.

(Professor Helmuth described Esmarch's new method of preventing hemorrhage in amputations.)

Necrosis still showing in the stump, although the operation was well performed. Mal-nutrition of bone the cause. ℞. silicea, 30, once a day.

Specific Ulcer.

JANE S., *Aged Twenty-seven Years.*

Six years ago fell upon her knee. Immediately afterwards there were no alarming symptoms, but in a short time the knee began to enlarge, and the disease commonly denominated *white swelling* resulted. This state continued until one year ago, when an ulcer appeared on the anterior surface of the leg, below the patella. This ulcer has now reached the size of a man's hand, and is spreading rapidly. Has profuse fetid discharge. Patient has bone pains at night and headache; has had sore throat, and had, some time since, an ulcer at ankle joint of opposite leg. The appearance of the ulcer, together with the above symptoms, are sufficient indications of syphilitic taint.

Prescribed iodide of potash, grs. ij., four times a day internally, and topical application of carbolic acid spray (Lister's sol.). In this case the constitutional taint was inherited from the father. Among the antidotes for the syphilitic poison iodide of potash is certainly one of the very best.

Double Scrotal Hernia.

J. E. H., *Aged Five Years*,

has double oblique inguinal hernia, which has become scrotal. Cough impulse perceptible, tumor opaque, congenital. Hernia may be confounded with hydrocele, which may also be congenital. The following are a few of the points of differential diagnosis:

Cong. Hernia.	Hydrocele.
1. Appears from the top of scrotum.	1. Appears first at bottom of scrotum.
2. Is generally opaque.	2. Is more or less translucent.
3. Has cough impulse.	3. Has none.
4. Testicle felt at bottom of scrotum, distinct from tumor.	4. Testicle scarcely felt, if at all.

The testicle, in its descent through the ingunial canal, may lodge at the ring and simulate hernia. To determine whether this be the case, interrogate the scrotum. Taxis was employed, and the hernia readily reduced. An appropriate truss was ordered, and nux vom. given internally.

Necrosis of the Os Frontis.

Geo. R. M., *Aged Fifty-one Years.*

About twenty months ago there appeared, from constitutional causes, at a point one and a half inches above left temple, an abscess, which increased until it became the size of an egg. Slough came out, and the abscess remained open, suppuration continuing this morning a sequestrum about an inch square was discharged, consisting of the external table of the bone, the underlying diploe presenting healthy granulations, with profuse secretion of fetid pus.

Ordered the parts dressed with Lister's sol. carb. acid, and to be taken internally, silicea 200. Care must be exercised to keep the hair from the wound in all injuries to parts covered with hair.

Hypertrophy of Mamma in Boy.

John W., *Aged Nine Years.*

Two years ago, without known cause, the left breast began to enlarge, with burning, stinging pains, worse at night and in damp weather. The breast is soft, and nearly as large as a woman's. There is neither hardness nor soreness.

Phos. 30 was prescribed, it being peculiarly adapted to such cases.

Pustular Eruption.

Eliza A., *Aged Seventeen Years.*

Has pustular eruption on middle finger of right hand, caused by wearing a ring. Eruption appeared about two years ago. Commences as pustules, which degenerate into a squamous condition. Burns after scratching. Resembles impetigo.

Sulphur every night and morning.

Encysted Hydrocele.

Harvey D., *Aged Six Years.*

The tumor in scrotum was first noticed about three months ago. There is no cough impulse; testicle distinctly felt at bottom of scrotum; translucency distinct when applying a lighted taper; the pains are paroxysmal, so that he screams during motion. Exploring needle is followed by exuding of serous fluid. Hydrocele in children may be cured by puncturing, to allow escape of fluid and the internal administration of medicine. In adults, however, an injection of iodine or a seton is usually necessary.

Prescribed rhododendron 30, night and morning. The sac was punctured and the fluid withdrawn.

Hypertrophy of the Clitoris.

MARTHA P., *Aged Thirty Years.*

Been married three years; has three children. Contracted syphilis from her husband. This case is a most remarkable one. The nymphæ are enormously enlarged, and project beyond the external labia, which are also swollen. The clitoris is singularly cylindrical in shape, having a length of three inches and a diameter of one and one half inches. Several pedunculated condylomatous growths, varying in length from one to three inches, appear, arising from the labia minora. The perineum is thickly studded with these growths, which extend backward to the anus. Complicated with this affection are painful external hemorrhoids. Goes for weeks without an evacuation and is in constant distress. Prescribed thuya 3, gtt. v. three times a day, topically:

℞ Thuya, ʒ j.
Aquæ, ℥ vj.
M.

Farinaceous diet ordered, also sitz bath night and morning, after which the above application is to be made. Must be kept quiet and in recumbent position. If these means are not productive of good, surgical measures will be resorted to. The use of nitric acid and the bichloride of mercury in the treatment of such diseases was pointed out.

Bursa at little finger dissected out, it not having yielded to previous treatment. Crepitation at wrist gone.

Exostosis of Inf. Max.

MRS. P., *Aged Thirty-four Years.*

About a year ago there came a swelling on left side of face, just anterior to and below the ear, accompanied by neuralgic pains, which were worse in damp weather. Has earache constantly. Has had diseased teeth, which were extracted. It was very sensitive, especially at one point. Has grown steadily to the present time.

Prescribed Hecla lava 3, three powders daily for a week.

There are two forms of exostosis—cancellated and ivory; the former usually attacking the epiphyses of the long bones; the latter, by far the most formidable, appears in the flat bones, especially those of the head and face. The causes are constitutional, rarely local. In the case above cited the predisposition already existing (the decayed teeth) may have been the exciting cause, while the neuralgia may have been the result of pressure of the tumor upon the nerves of the part.

Necrosis.

GEO. PIERCE (*Sailor*), *Aged Fifty-one Years.*

(*Continued from page* 181.)

For the last week has not been improving. Is alternately better and worse. Within the past two weeks several spiculæ of bone have been discharged from the wound. Were these portions larger, the indications would be more favorable. Recommends scraping the bone. To which patient objects.

Prescribed silicea.

Pott's Fracture.

CHAS. J., *Aged Twenty-six Years.*

Right leg injured three months ago by falling plank. Began to swell, the swelling going and coming every week. There is considerable pain, which is greater in damp weather. Has had a fracture of the lower third of the fibula, with partial rotation of the astragalus, and rupture of external lateral ligament. The foot is somewhat everted. There is some deformity and stiffness of the joint. Ordered an elastic stocking for the leg, and prescribed arnica externally and internally. The prolonged use of too strong a solution of arnica will often produce a condition closely resembling erysipelas.

Anchylosis.

MARY BEAUMET, *Aged Sixteen Years.*

(*Continued from page* 180 *and to page* 83.)

The operation has been productive of great good. Can now masticate her food, which she has not done for nine years. Cicatrix remains, which in time it will probably be necessary to dissect out. Movement of the jaw must be kept up, and to prevent contraction she must have inserted between her teeth wedges of hickory wood. Dec. 6, much improved.

Sebaceous Cyst.

MRS. S., *Aged Forty-two Years.*

(*Continued from page* 174.)

The tumor at middle third of clavicle, which one month ago had the appearance of and was diagnosed as enchondroma, has now become much more yielding, and is thought to be a sebaceous cyst. It was carefully dissected out, yet with some difficulty, as it penetrated to within dangerous proximity to subclavian vessels. Another method of removal is by suppuration, which can be induced by means of seton. Wound dressed with carbolic acid.

Needle in Wrist.

KATE M., *Aged Twenty Years.*

Two weeks since a crochet needle entered radial side of wrist and was broken off. An effort had been made to remove it but failed. She comes now to the clinic. The needle cannot be felt. Was directed to allow it to remain, under the supposition that it may make its appearance at the surface, when it could be easily removed. The point of exit and point of entrance of such bodies are often widely apart. It is useless in this case to make incisions around the point of its entrance.

Tongue-Tie.

ANDREW B., *Aged Five Years.*

Can protrude the tongue quite well. Can only speak the word "mamma." Examination shows frænum too short. Care must be exercised in performing this apparently trivial operation: first, lest dangerous hemorrhage occur, and second, lest a too free incision allow the tongue to fall backward, producing suffocation. Cases are recorded where death has resulted from each of these causes.

The operation can be performed with either a curved steel-pointed bistoury or with probe-pointed scissors. If a bistoury is used, cut from behind and forward.

Operation performed with a bistoury.

Phymosis.

JOHN C. M., *Aged Thirty-seven Years.*

Acquired phymosis. Cannot retract the prepuce at all. Is of several years' standing. Has produced spermatorrhœa. Operation performed by drawing forward the prepuce, and with the scissors cutting it across. The mucous membrane was then trimmed off, and the cut surfaces of integument and mucous membrane approximated by means of silver wire sutures, so that adhesions would then unite the mucous with the cutaneous surfaces. Among the causes of phymosis are wounds, gonorrhœa, syphilis and balanitis.

Paraphymosis is a state exactly opposite to the preceding; is often caused by the successful retraction of phymotic prepuce; or, as with phymosis, it may be caused by gonorrhœa or chancroids. If this condition is allowed to continue gangrene may result. Paraphymosis can often be reduced in the following manner: After a thorough application of sweet oil, place the ends of the thumbs against the glands, in front, while the index fingers are pressed upon the prepuce laterally behind the point of constriction. Then, by bringing the fingers forward, while the thumbs exert a counter-force upon the glans, the reduction is accomplished. When reduction cannot otherwise be performed, slitting through the point of constriction may be resorted to.

Fistula in Cheek.

MARY M., *Aged Eight Years.*

Fistulous opening on right cheek, caused by scrofula, with enlargement of the glands of the neck. Pus exudes; face pale; has scrofulous cachexia. Has pain, which is worse at night. Loses flesh. In persons afflicted with scrofula, there is always a tendency to leucothæmia. Probe discovers no caries. Prescribed calc. 30, twice daily. Baryta also is often indicated in this condition.

Condylomata and Enlarged Clitoris.

MARTHA PINCKNEY, *Aged Thirty Years.*

(*Continued from page* 185.)

This was a peculiarly aggravated case of condylomata and enlarged clitoris and labia, which were so large as to completely cover the vaginal and anal openings and the perineum; they were from the size of a bean to that of an egg, and, if removed, would have filled a two quart measure. The patient was born in Virginia, was married to a man from whom she had contracted syphilis, to whom she bore three children; she was finally compelled to leave him on account of his vices. Strange to say, however, this woman was earning her living at service, being obliged to stand upon her feet most of the time; she suffered terrible pain during urination, with severe aching in her bones, chiefly at night. She was also much exhausted from the bleeding of the tumors. The condylomata and the clitoris were pedunculated and covered with unhealthy mucus, and, owing to the irritation consequent upon walking, were constantly bleeding.

She was ordered (until she could be received into the hospital) to have frequent sitz baths, farinaceous food, no meat, compresses saturated with one part of tincture of thuja to eight parts of water externally, and thuja 3d internally, gtt. iii. three times a day.

Attention was called to the use of the following agents for the refibroid tumors, hemorrhoids, condylomata, and other soft parts, viz: the *ecraseur*, invented by Chassaignac, *nitric acid*, *mercurius corrosivus* (ʒ j. to ℥ j. collodion) and the *galvano-caustic* wire, after which, the patient being etherized, the enlarged clitoris was removed by the ecraseur with no subsequent homorrhage; two small candylomata beneath the clitoris were then ligated with a double thread and cut off by the scissors.

These two ligatures and the one through the pedicle of the clitoris were left in, to guard against secondary hemorrhage. The patient was then placed in the hospital and the previous treatment continued.

The patient was reported to be doing well.

The patient, being etherized, was placed in Sims' position, and three anal condylomata were ligated with a double thread and cut off with the scissors.

Two large condylomata were ligated and left to slough away; they were all found to be very tough and vascular; it was then ordered that the wounds be dressed at once with cold water, then for two days with styptic cotton, which is cotton dipped into a solution of tannin, persulphate of iron, benzoic acid and alum. Only three condylomata now remained.

Prof. Helmuth reported that the patient was doing very well, and that he had searched the records and found but few similar cases, and these were not so severe as this.

Scrofulous Enlargement of Parotid Gland.

MARY J. M., *Agent Eight Years.*

This child was light haired, pale faced, nervous, puffy under the eyes, had dilated pupils and presented a general scrofulous appearance, though the parents and the other children were said to be in fair health.

Eight weeks ago a hard swelling appeared under the right inferior maxillary, causing the child to cry a great deal, chiefly at night, which finally discharged pus externally, since which time she has lost flesh. She has had no other glandular swellings, neither has she been salivated. There was no disease of the bone, but simply a scrofulous enlargement of the parotid gland. Air, exercise, and calcarb. 30th, a powder three times a day, were ordered.

Sprain.

ANTHONY W., *Aged Fifteen Years.*

This lad suffered from a sprain of his left ankle with severe, deep pain, occurring without any known cause, unless due to a slight mis-step eight weeks ago; he had suffered eight weeks since with rheumatism.

A sprain was described as an accidental rupture or wrenching of the parts about the joint, often with dislocation suddenly taking place which the muscles at once reduce. The patient had, probably, from subacute arthritis, weakened the joint, thus predisposing to the accident.

There was neither a fracture nor a rupture of the internal lateral ligaments. Having been preceded by disease of the joint it was ordered that he rest as much as possible, using a crutch when it was necessary for him to walk; he should not touch his foot to the ground for six weeks, and must not be exposed to dampness or be out at night. A cold compress was applied at night, covered by flannel and oiled silk, and rhus tox. 3d. gtts. x. in half a glass of water, a table spoonful every three hours was ordered.

He was told that if not properly taken care of, effusion in the joint might result and finally fibrous anchylosis.

Obstruction of Nasal Passages.

ERNEST D., *aged 7 months.*

This babe presents a peculiar case: its mother states that the child snores "terribly" and has great difficulty in breathing during sleep and nursing; when sucking the respirations can be heard all over the room. Attention was called to the fact that any obstruction in the posterior portion of the mouth, as swelling of the tonsils or a polypus, or an enlargement of the turbinated bones, might cause obstruction to breathing. The tonsils or velum palati did not seem enlarged, and an attempt was made to pass a small bougie into the nostrils, which failed; a small probe was, however, with effort passed to the posterior nares of either side, and it was found that the turbinated bones were enlarged and the schneiderian membrane thickened, thus closing the passages. The mother was instructed to use a syringe with a fine nozzle to throw warm water through the nares, and have the probing repeated every week or two, gradually increasing the size of the instrument, and Hecla-lava was ordered to be administered at night.

Section of the Nerve and Tendon of the Thumb.

MARY B., *Aged Nineteen Years.*

Three years ago a playmate pushed a barbed crochet needle from over the extensor tendon of the right thumb through to the inner and fleshy side of the thumb. Her physician broke off the protruding barb and drew the needle back through the point of entrance. Since then she has suffered with pain in the thumb during bad weather, and with frequently recurring numbness. It was pronounced that the nerve and tendon of the thumb had been divided, and a simple electrical apparatus was ordered to be used once or twice a day as follows: apply a ring of zinc around the thumb and one of copper around the wrist, connect these with a copper wire and put a little vinegar under the copper ring. This is also an excellent appliance in bed sores and obstinate ulcers.

Varicocele.

C. M., *Aged Twenty-two Years.*

An operation for varicocele being about to take place, the following very opportune explanation of varicocele and its operations was given:

The tunica vaginalis is a peritoneal investment of the spermatic cord and testicle: the spermatic cord is made up of the spermatic artery and veins, and vas deferens, the latter carrying the semen to the *vesiculæ seminales;* the pampiniform plexus is the collection of veins which pass through the spermatic cord.

Varicocele usually occurs on the left side, because the right spermatic vein enters the vena cava acendens at an acute angle, while the left spermatic vein enters the efferent vein of the kidney at a right angle, and also the valves of the right vein do not open as readily as those of the left.

The *symptoms* of varicocele are, a feeling of weight in the testes, pain in the small of the back, and a depressed mental condition; the patients usually are strong, robust young men, of good habits, accustomed to hard work and long continued standing.

The *treatment* is palliative and radical. The first is by means of a suspensory bandage. The second aims to obliterate the enlarged veins by either of the following methods, viz:

1st. Pass a needle armed with a cord behind the vein, making the point of exit of the needle near the point of entrance; then twist the ends of the cord and you thus compress the veins. Thirteen of fourteen cases treated in this way were cured; the fourteenth died of phlebitis.

2d. Remove a crescentic piece of the scrotum, then sew up the wound and thus cause compression.

3d. Make an incision through the scrotum and ligate the veins.

4th. Inject perchloride of iron.

5th. Put a truss and pad over the external abdominal ring through which the veins pass up, and by this means irritate the veins and effect a cure.

That method is the best which excludes the air from the veins. It must, also, be borne in mind that ligating the spermatic artery will result in atrophy of the testis, and this accident has occurred to distinguished surgeons, one of whom was murdered for having made a mistake and included the spermatic arteries in his ligature. It is better, then, remembering that the vas deferens feels like a ligamentous cord; that the artery can be known by its gentle pulsation, and the veins by their feeling like a bundle of earth worms,

6th. To get the vas deferens between the thumb of the left hand and the os pubis; the artery between the first and second fingers, thus leaving the veins clear for ligation as follows: pass a curved needle armed with a double thread with the loop near the eye of the needle, in front of the thumb through the integument behind the veins; cause it to reappear in front of the first finger and remove the needle; then enter the unthreaded needle at the same point of entrance as before, carry it just beneath the scrotal wall and cause it to emerge at the same point of exit as before; then slip the loop over the point of the needle and tie the loose ends of the cord over the other end of the needle; if you have been successful, the veins alone are included between the cord behind and the needle in front and you can compress lightly for four days and then more tightly for about ten days longer; if you have, unfortunately, included with the veins the artery or the vas deferens, and discover it within these four days, no harm is done, for the removal of the needle restores everything to its original position. As minor points, have your patients wear no suspensory bandage for a few hours previous to the operation, and also take exercise before the operation to fill the veins; also, have corks placed on the ends of the needles to prevent injury to the scrotum. After these remarks the patient was etherized and the last described operation was successfully performed.

Epithelioma of the Tongue.

GEO. H., *Aged Forty-three Years.*

This man presented a very interesting case; his tongue became sore on the right side a year ago, and a white vesicle was noticed which he tried to pick off with a knife; he then took a caustic and burned it off two or three times, making it worse. A physician gave him tannin to apply which much aggravated the disease, though he was assured it would cure him promptly. Since then he had used iodide of potash internally. Five weeks ago ulceration began with stinging pains through the tongue, chiefly at night and in swallowing. Since this time he had used arsenicum, which relieved the pains in ten minutes after it was taken. The ulcerated surface is now about an inch and a quarter long, and one half inch deep and has bled once only. It was found that he had always been in health, excepting while suffering from a chancre, nineteen years ago. He had chewed and smoked tobacco, using pipes with amber mouth pieces and also the common clay pipe, the latter causing often a stinging pain; he has ceased, however, the use of both coffee and tobacco.

The disease was diagnosed as an epithelioma, and since arsenicum 30 seemed so well adapted, he was ordered to continue it, a powder three times a day, unless it became worse, requiring removal by the ecraseur or galvano caustic wire. Bread and milk, mush, rice and hominy, and mutton broth were ordered, and to wash the ulcer with warm water. This patient returned to the hospital to have the entire tongue removed, but before the appointed time, left without assigning any reason.

Oblique Inguinal Hernia.

RANDOLPH R., *Aged Eleven Years.*

This child had a swelling which appeared suddenly in his scrotum five months ago, and no effort had been made by his parents to have it attended to, though it had sometimes become "almost black." It gave cough impulse, hence was not encysted hydrocele of the cord; it was not infantile, because the testicle was at the bottom and was pronounced a congenital oblique inguinal hernia still reducible. The gut was returned without difficulty, and it was ordered that the child wear a truss and have nux vom.^{30th}, a powder every night, to strengthen the muscles of the abdominal wall.

Partial Paralysis.

J. BURNS, *Aged Four Years.*

This man reports that he began to suffer with stinging pains in his hips during walking three years ago; in the course of a year his right leg became a little lame, and is now smaller and shorter than the other; his leg "goes to sleep" and becomes cold very easily; he is unable to raise his foot, and suffers with severe pains shooting down the anterior surface of the leg. His symptoms are all worse in damp weather, and his appetite very poor. His physician had called it sciatica, cupped him, and gave him medicine with no benefit; he has also used *rhus tox.* for ten days without effect. He had never had a blow upon his back or a strain, nor suffered with pain in the knee.

It was pronounced a threatened paralysis, and electricity to be the best treatment, but, since we are unable to furnish him with this for the present, he was given colocynth to be taken every fifteen minutes during his severe pains, and ordered to moisten a flannel rag in alcohol, having a tablesponful of salt to the pint, and to rub his leg with this night and morning, also to take plenty of out door exercise.

The internal medicines were rhus tox. at first, and afterward strychnine.

Colles' Fracture.

DAVID G., *Aged Seventeen Years.*

This young man had fallen through a hatchway ten weeks ago, and sustained a Colles' fracture, viz., a fracture of the lower extremity of the radius, with dislocation of the ulna, which had been treated with a pistol splint, and he probably came to see if it had been properly managed. He was told that it was not necessary to break the bone over again, and that time, friction and exercise would help him regain the normal motion of the joint.

Hydrocele.

J. L. S., *Aged Thirty-eight Years.*

The following diagnosis of hydrocele and description of the methods of cure were made before the operation. Hydrocele of the tunica vaginalis is a collection of serous fluid between the tunica vaginalis testis and the tunica communis.

This man's trouble began seven years ago, and is a *hydrocele*, because the swelling began at the bottom; it gives no cough impulse, he has severe pains in the back and groin, is very depressed, mentally; the tumor is translucent and irreducible; while *hernia* comes from above, has cough impulse, can usually be reduced by taxis, and is opaque.

Varicocele, on the other hand, has the peculiar earth worm feeling of the veins.

Some cases of hydrocele can be cured in youth by medicine, and encysted hydrocele of the cord in infants will often spontaneously disappear. The methods of cure mentioned were by, 1st. *Seton*: Insert a trocar and draw off the fluid; then push the trocar upward through the scrotum, withdraw the trocar, leaving in the canula, through which pass a cord; then having withdrawn the canula, tie the loose ends of the cord. 2d. *Injection*. Iodine can be injected into the tunica vaginalis, causing sufficient inflammation to cure; or still better is the injection:

℞ Iodide of Potash, ℨ ij.
Water, ℥ ss.
Tincture of Iodine, ℨ iv.
M.

3d. *Incision*. An incision can be made through the scrotum, and the fluid drawn off; this sometimes is sufficient.

4th. *Electrolysis*. 5th. *The Aspirator*. This instrument consists of a graduated glass jar having two rubber tubes of three feet each. At the extremity of each of these tubes is attached a brass piece furnishing a thread on the end and a stopcock; each aspirator is furnished with a set of capillary needles, that screw on to one of the brass pieces mentioned, and has also a small brass air pump which is attached to the other brass piece.

Operation. Attaching a needle to one rubber tube, the air pump to the other, close the stopcock next to the needle and open the one next to the air pump; work the piston of the pump, which exhausts the air from the jar and tubes, then, having inserted the needle in any fluid tumor (in this case the scrotum), the contents of the tumor are forced into the previously formed vacuum of the jar: the puncture of the needle being capillary, no air can enter the exhausted cavity, and the operation can be repeated without injury. In this case the last mentioned injection was used (after the evacuation of the sixteen ounces of yellow and thick fluid of the hydrocele) by an improvement of Prof. Helmuth's on the aspirator. To the needle used, had been added a stopcock at its posterior extremity; after the withdrawal of the fluid from the scrotum, this stopcock was closed and the aspirator tube unscrewed from the needle and taken away; a brass syringe charged with the injection was then screwed to the needle, the stopcock on the needle opened, the injection forced in and allowed to remain two minutes; the injection was then drawn back into the syringe, and the needle was withdrawn from the scrotum, and thus the whole operation, consisting of the *removal* of the contents of the tumor, the *injection* into the cavity, and the *removal* of the injection, was accomplished by one capillary puncture.

Lithotomy.

JOHN D., *Aged Four Years.*

This boy had been troubled with a vesical calculus, which had become lodged in the prostatic portion of the urethra, causing great difficulty in urination, and at times suppression ; there was danger of rupture of the urethra and extravasation of urine; his prepuce was elongated, symptomatic of calculus, and he had also the frequent inclination to urinate which belongs to the disease.

As to the operation: If possible the stone was to be removed through the urethra by a fine pair of urethra forceps. The patient was etherized and the extracton attempted, but it was unsuccessful; recourse was then had to the removal through the perineum, which was successfully done by the lateral operation, and a stone the size of a bean removed; the incision was made high up in the perineum on account of the position of the calculus; some little difficulty was experienced in securing a small deep artery, cut during the operation.

After the operation the boy was removed from the hospital.

Jan. 17th. Prof. Helmuth reported that on the 12th inst. the boy had been removed without his knowledge to his home in New Jersey, and that, as soon as he discovered it, he had written to a physician there to see him daily and report. He had done so, and all went well till the 16th inst., when it was found there was infiltration of urine into the tissues of the scrotum, which were purplish in color.

The Professor had him returned to the hospital, and he finds that he passes about one half of his urine this morning through the urethra. It was ordered that the scrotum be strapped up by adhesive plaster attached to the abdomen, and he be carefully watched. The Professor stated that it was possible for one to recover after losing one half the scrotum from this cause. No catheter was to be used in this case.

Jan. 24th. After the scrotum had been strapped up a very small amount of urine escaped through the perineal wound for three days, since which none had escaped, and the purplish spot was nearly gone.

Attention was called to the fact that there is more danger of infiltration of urine when the triangular ligament is divided, as in this operation, than in other operations for the urethral calculus.

Jan. 31st. At this time all the urine was passed through the urethra, the purplish appearance of the scrotum was all gone, and the boy prenounced cured.

Popliteal Aneurism,

Cured by Digital Compression in 72 Hours.

CHAS. D. (colored), *Aged Fifty Years.*

Before this man was brought into the theatre, attention was called to the following particulars:

An aneurism is a tumor containing blood and communicating with the cavity of an artery. The ordinary or encysted aneurism is sub-divided into several classes, thus; it is called *fusiform*, when the whole circumference of the artery was expanded; *pedunculated*, when there is a small opening between the aneurism and the artery; *true*, when all the coats of the artery are expanded; *false*, where the internal and middle coats are upturned; *diffuse*, when the sac walls are formed by cellular tissue; *dissecting*, when the blood passes between the coats of the artery. Any sudden and rapid strain of a joint may give rise to an aneurism; a clot forms on the wall of the sac, becoming almost organized, which thickens the coat of the artery and is called after Brocca, the *active clot;* this sometimes proceeds to such an extent as to cure the aneurism and is *Nature's* method of cure. The "*passive clot*" is a currant jelly-like substance found in the centre of the aneurism. The method of cure of *Antyllus*, which is the oldest, is to ligate the artery above and below the aneurism, cut down on the sac and empty it of its contents. *Anel's* method was to ligate the artery on the cardiac side near the aneurism. *Hunter's* method was to ligate the artery on the cardiac side at some distance from the aneurism. *Wardrop* and *Brasdors'* method was to ligate the artery on the distal side of the aneurism. Other methods are by *tourniquet* to arrest the flow of blood from behind and thus allow a fibrinous clot to form and obliterate the sac. Both a single and double ball tourniquet have been used, but the latter is the better, as it allows a change of pressure from one spot to another and thus relieves the patient. The *manipulation method* is devised to compel the "*active clot*" to change its position, to enlarge, fill up and obliterate the sac. Sometimes *ulceration* and *sloughing* occurs spontaneously in the aneurismal tumor. *Forced flexion; acupressure*, used by Sir James Simpson, and *digital compression* are all employed by surgeons at the present day, but the latter method, when there are intelligent assistants at hand, is the *best*. This compression may be continued from four to seventy-five hours, as may be necessary; one case at least is on record where the patient effected a cure by compression with his own hands in four or five hours.

Strange to say popliteal aneurism often occurs in negroes, and the *symptoms* are, after undue exertion of the leg, a sudden pain, snap and faintness, and a pulsating tumor is found in the popliteal space; sometimes a fibrinous clot forms on the walls of the sac, making the pulsation less distinct and even finally imperceptible. If the ear is applied over the aneurism, a blowing or rasping sound is heard, called the *bruit;* the pressure on the surrounding veins causes them to become varicose. This man was in the habit of carrying a heavy sick woman from her carriage to her room; on one occasion he felt a snap and a severe pain down his left leg, and found the next day a tumor behind his knee and the veins of the leg swollen and the leg stiff.

Pulsation could not now be felt very distinctly, on account of the active clot.

Thirty of the class having volunteered to make digital compression as long as necessary for the cure of this case, they were divided into six classes of five each, each class to remain on duty three hours and each member to compress twelve minutes of each hour. Pressure was begun at 6 P. M.; patient's temperature in the axilla at this time way 98½°, the temperature of the tumor was 96, and his pulse was beating 80 per minute. 8 P. M. pulse came up to 88, at 9 P. M. going back to 80; the pain at this time became unbearable, requiring the use of morphine. At 11.40 P. M. he was seized with severe rigors lasting but a short time, his temperature running down to $94\frac{1}{2}°$ and his pulse to 81, remaining till morning between 71 and 76.

JAN. 11th. At 8 A. M. his pulse came up to 84, and his temperature to $98\frac{1}{2}°$; by noon the pulse reached 94. Only slight pulsation could now be detected in the tumor. At 3 P. M. the pulse was 104, decreasing gradually, reaching 88. At 5.40 P. M. the patient was quiet and suffering no pain. At 6 P. M. pressure was taken off for a moment, the pulsation found to be very slight and a movable clot plainly discernible. Between 9 P. M. and morning the patient slept a little during each pressure, waking at every change; at 10.30 P. M. there was some *subsultus tendinum*.

JAN. 12th. At 1 A. M. the patient's temperature was $98\frac{1}{2}°$, pulse 100 which decreased to 92 by 6 A. M. At 3.15 A. M. there was further *subsultus tendinum;* at 9 A. M. his pulse was 94, his temperature $99\frac{1}{4}°$ and that of the tumor $94\frac{1}{4}°$, and he was suffering no pain. At 3 P. M. his pulse was 105: at 4 P. M. it was 98 and temperature of the tumor $96\frac{3}{8}°$. At 6 P. M. his temperature was $99\frac{3}{8}°$ and that of the tumor $98\frac{3}{4}$.

JAN. 13th. At 4 A. M. his pulse was 91, gradually reducing to 84 by 6 A. M., when his temperature was 99° and that of the tumor $98\frac{1}{2}°$. At 3 P. M. his pulse was 92, his temperature $99\frac{1}{4}°$ and that of the tumor $96\frac{1}{2}°$. At 9 A. M. his pulse was 82, his temperature $98\frac{1}{2}°$ and that of the aneurism $98\frac{1}{2}°$, at which time, after 75 hours' pressure, it was discontinued. Prof. Helmuth had taken great interest in the case, visiting the patient daily at 9 A. M., noon and midnight, and leaving nothing undone that could contribute to success. Great credit was due the class for their kindness and attention. The patient slept well all night and woke in good condition, though exhausted.

JAN. 14th. The tumor was carefully examined by Prof. Helmuth, Thompson and Robinson, Drs. Baldwin and McVicar, and others, and no pulsation could be detected, and the tumor was found to be gradually reducing and hardening; the collateral circulation had been growing better day by day, and was now very well established, pulsation being distinct in the articular arteries. An examination was made daily and no pulsation detected.

JAN. 17th. Prof. Helmuth reported in the clinic that he regarded the patient as cured; but, for fear there was a small stream passing through the sac, ordered pressure to be resumed on the 18th at 9 A. M. and kept up for 12 hours, to be again resumed on the 19th at 9 A. M., and kept up for twelve hours, which was done. Up to the 24th inst. no pulsation could be detected, the tumor was two thirds gone, and the patient was brought into the amphitheatre and questioned. In reply, he stated that he had been walking around for two days and felt no pain in the knee, whereas before the operation for weeks he had suffered most terrible agony, had been unable to lie down at all, or put his foot on the ground, and had used opium and every thing he could get, to relieve his pain, without any relief.

He was instructed to go home on the 26th and to keep up pressure every morning and night for fifteen minutes, and to return in three weeks; and was pronounced cured. On the 26th Prof. Helmuth came to the hospital with his carriage to take the patient home, for fear he might injure himself if he went home on the crowded street cars, and found the patient had climbed over the transom of the door of his room, and, taking a crowded car, had fled.

FEB. 2d. Prof. Helmuth reported that the patient was able to put his heel within a half inch of the ground, was able to work, and was earning his living.

Empyema.

W. H. POST, *Aged Forty-one Years.*

This gentleman was sent here by his physician to satisfy himself that his diagnosis was correct. A year and a half ago he had typhoid fever: a year ago his right breast became hard and sore, and then discharged freely both blood and pus for three months, but during the last nine months pus alone; neither air nor bits of bone had ever been discharged at any time; he had been in good health for months and was getting fleshy. The probe entered the opening beneath the nipple an inch and a quarter. It was pronounced Empyema, and silicea was ordered.

Bursa.

MARY H., *Aged Sixteen Years.*

Adventitious bursa of ulnar side of left wrist. Contains transparent fluid. Passed a seton.

Nævus.

MATILDA B., *Aged Eleven Years.*

Attention was first called to the following operation for nævi: 1st. *Electrolysis*, which is not always successful. 2d. By placing two pins at right angles beneath the nævus and ligating it with thread beneath the pins, being careful to insert and withdraw the pins in sound tissue, which causes less hemorrhage aud insures better success. 3d. By Perchloride of Iron. 4th. By Nitric Acid. 5th. By Pressure. 6th. By Vaccination. 7th. By a thread soaked in Nitric Acid and drawn through. 8th. By passing two cords beneath the nævus in one direction, two others beneath it at right angles to the former two, then tying and constricting the nævus in quarters and allowing it to slough away. This being a typical case, operated on once before by electrolysis unsuccessfully, the last mentioned method was employed after etherization. Attention was called to the use of nitric acid to cauterize any twigs that may reappear: if done at once it avoids another operation; also to the fact that some nævi are so large as to occupy one side of the face and require the ligation of the common carotid; also to the primary and transient anæsthesia caused by ether very soon after its administration, during which minor and brief operations can often be performed, and the secondary and more profound anæsthesia following.

JAN. 24th. Patient was brought in doing nicely; the mother was instructed to dress it with simple cerate and return to the Dispensary in three days.

Aneurism.

ISAAC R., *Aged Fifty-one Years.*

This was a case that has given rise to some discussion among surgeons, and the man has been before all prominent American surgeons and in many College Clinics. He carried certificates from many surgeons, most of whom pronounced it an aneurism of the thoracie and abdominal costa, and with these certificates he was able to secure a living. His history and symptoms were as follows: two and a half years ago he was working at his trade, steel pen making, when he noticed a swelling in his back which annoyed him in lying down, causing a choking feeling and increasing till he had fainting spells; his abdomen then began to swell, chiefly on the left side, and he began to pass blood with his stool. He now passes about three table spoonfuls with every stool, cannot lie down at all, and is about the size of a woman with child at term.

Attention was again called to the subject of aneurism—to the *false* variety, where the external coat only of the artery is expanded, the internal and middle being ruptured, to the *true* variety where all the coats are expanded, to the *dissecting*, where the blood passes between the laminæ of the middle coat usually, after passing down the course of the artery, rupturing the internal coat and connecting again with the circulation. Prof. Helmuth expressed the belief that this was a dissecting aneurism; one peculiarity of the case was that no pulsation could be felt. The man is liable to death at any moment, but may yet outlive his physicians.

Hydrocele and Hernia.

C. W. S., *Aged Three Months.*

The mother of this baby, who seemed perfectly posted as to the case, stated that when the child was three weeks old she first noticed that it had a hydrocele on the right side, and that a rupture descended every four or five days, swelling the scrotum like an egg and causing the child much pain; she was about to have a truss fitted to the child, thinking that it would cure both affections. Examination showed translucency and that it was not a hydrocele of the tunica vaginalis, because the scrotum could be drawn down readily and was not evenly distended, but was an encysted hydrocele of the cord accompanied by oblique inguinal hernia. An exploring needle was very carefully used and the fluid drawn off, which will probably excite sufficient inflammation to produce a cure; and she was instructed to have a truss fitted after two or three days.

INDEX.

www.ingramcontent.com/pod-product-compliance
Lightning Source LLC
LaVergne TN
LVHW011211110826
845150LV00006B/1395

9781425517700